BECOMING
ALL
YOU

CAN

BE

**A PERSONAL GROWTH JOURNEY TO AWAKENING,
TRANSFORMATION, AND WISDOM**

Praise for *Becoming All You Can Be*

"While most of us spent our childhoods innocently playing hide-and-seek and Red Rover, eight-year-old Anela was awakened by flashing lights and the blare of loudspeakers and watched from her military housing complex as fathers in full combat gear rushed out the doors in the dead of night, leaving their children wondering if they would ever see their dads again.

Years later, at the age of twenty-three, as we were settling into the comfort of office jobs and cozy homes, Anela was leading her platoon under the blazing 120° heat in the middle of a combat zone in Somalia.

In this remarkable book, Anela shares her extraordinary journey and reveals the profound gifts she uncovered within every challenge. Through her wisdom and thought-provoking prompts, she encourages us to reflect deeply on our own lives and uncover the hidden treasures waiting there to be discovered."

—Debra Poneman, Founder, Yes to Success, Inc.
YestoSuccess.com

"Spending any meaningful time with Anela, one sees the *tour de force* she is in her life journey. Having the insights of lessons learned in the service—coupled with spiritual wisdom—offers an inspiring touchstone for anyone."

—John Newton, Ancestral Clearing and
Founder of Health Beyond Belief
healthbeyondbelief.com

"Anela Arcari's *Becoming All You Can Be* is a heartfelt tapestry of short stories and life lessons that encourage and uplift. Through embracing life's wonders and messages, Anela reminds us that life is what we make of it. Her reflections ignite hope and reveal our boundless capacity to create new possibilities and reach our highest potential. This book is a gem for anyone seeking a spark of encouragement and a reminder of their inner power."

—Joy Taylor, Companion Guide in Awakening
Author of *Inspired: 7 Wisdoms of a Soul-Inspired Life*
ASoulInspiredLife.com

"Engaging! Enlightening! Empowering! In *Becoming All You Can Be*, Anela Arcari shares a refreshingly authentic and relatable perspective on becoming the best version of you! Her inspiring real-life stories and insightful journaling suggestions give the reader direct access to their own healing life stories, insights, and inspirations. Anela is a true teacher who leads by example! She leaves her readers inspired to do the same by seeing our own life experiences as valuable growth opportunities that we can turn into stories that inspire others to become all we can be!"

—Gerise Pappas, Transformational Coach,
Enneagram and Internal Family Systems
Practitioner
gerisepappas.com

"Anela Arcari's *Becoming All You Can Be* is an inspiring and heartfelt guide to self-discovery and growth. Through her compelling storytelling and practical journaling prompts, Anela invites readers to reflect on their experiences and uncover the lessons that shape their journey. This book is a treasure for anyone ready to embrace transformation and awaken to their fullest potential. A beautiful blend of wisdom, resilience, and hope—this book is a gift to the soul."

—Judi Miller, #1 Bestseller and Multiple Award Winner
Author of *Perfect: A Path to Love, Forgiveness, and Transformation*
Judimiller.net

"Relatable, authentic, and profoundly inspiring, *Becoming All You Can Be* is a heartfelt book for anyone navigating life's transitions— whether you're a parent, a professional, or a veteran reflecting on your journey. Anela Arcari's wisdom shines through her poignant stories and intuitive journaling prompts, offering a powerful blend of deep self-discovery and opportunities for personal growth.

This book graciously invites you to use the adversity in your life as a catalyst to courageous authentic living. It's a must-read for anyone seeking clarity, connection, and personal growth."

—Veronica L. Nabizadeh, Esq.
Author of *Don't Throw in the Towel, Yet!: How to Stay Married by a Battle-Weary Wife*
marriagerelationshiprestart.com

"Fascinating! Revealing! Empowering! With *Becoming All You Can Be*, Anela Arcari writes a unique and telling memoir-like book of profound transformational lessons learned from her life growing up in a military family and her own military career. Full of surprising twists and turns, this book will captivate you till the end. You will carry these powerful stories with you forever as they elevate your own journey of becoming all YOU can be! I loved this book and you will too!"

—Karoleen Fober, Intuitive Business and Life Mastery Coach and Strategist, Speaker, Creator of the Intuition Mastery Accelerator Program
Author of *Opening to Divine Intervention: Expand and Strengthen Your Intuitive Abilities and Spiritual Connection*
karoleenfober.com

"Amazing, inspiring, insightful, and moving! Like a conversation with a wise and compassionate friend, Anela's words will energize you and inspire you to listen to and trust in your own life lessons on your path to *Becoming All You Can Be!*"

—Kat Wells, Award-winning Author of
There's Got to Be Something More: 21 Days to Create a More Abundant, Purposeful, and Joyful Life
KatWells.com

"*Becoming All You Can Be* weaves a rich tapestry of stories that highlight what is possible when we are willing to change perspectives and go with the flow. If you are wanting guidance on how to turn your life into an adventure rather than an ordeal, this is the book for you!"

—Cindy Anne Mathers, Cultural Humility Mentor
Author of *DELVE-ing into Cultural Humility:
How Respect and Deep Listening Can Heal a Nation*
growingwellbeing.com.au

BECOMING
ALL
YOU
CAN
BE

A PERSONAL GROWTH JOURNEY TO AWAKENING, TRANSFORMATION, AND WISDOM

ANELA ARCARI

Capucia LLC
211 Pauline Drive #513
York, PA 17402
www.capuciapublishing.com
Send questions to: support@capuciapublishing.com

Paperback ISBN: 979-8-9920502-3-3
eBook ISBN: 979-8-9920502-4-0
Library of Congress Control Number: 2024927102

Cover Design: Ranilo Cabo
Layout: Ranilo Cabo
Author Photo: Lauren Mudrock
Editor and Proofreader: Karen Burton
Book Midwife: Karen Everitt

Printed in the United States of America

Capucia LLC is proud to be a part of the Tree Neutral® program. Tree Neutral offsets the number of trees consumed in the production and printing of this book by taking proactive steps such as planting trees in direct proportion to the number of trees used to print books. To learn more about Tree Neutral, please visit treeneutral.com.

DISCLAIMER

The purpose of this book is not to dispense medical advice or prescribe the use of any technique as a form of treatment for physical, emotional, or medical problems without the advice of a professional, either directly or indirectly. The intent of the author is to offer information of a general nature to help the reader in the quest for well-being. In the event the reader uses any of the information in this book for self or others, the author and the publisher assume no responsibility for the actions of the reader.

This book contains true stories and events. The author has shared these as accurately as memory will allow while acknowledging that memory is an imperfect recorder of history. In order to protect anonymity for persons both living and deceased, many names have been changed.

For all the brave women and men who stand ready to defend our precious freedom.
For all who bravely seek transformation and step forward to become all they can be.

Butterflies are beautiful, but the process of emerging from the chrysalis and spreading your wings can hurt like f**king hell. But still, you will survive the transformation (over and over again), and you will fly. Remember this when it hurts the most. This is the metamorphosis, the going down to liquid, and the rising again. It's no joke—but damn, it's one hell of a journey.

— Jeanette LeBlanc

CONTENTS

Foreword

As a PhD performance psychologist specializing in non-clinical practice, reflecting on the journey that brought me to this point inevitably leads me to moments of profound gratitude for those who have shaped my path. Among them towers Anela Arcari—a mentor, teacher, and friend whose guidance has profoundly influenced both my personal and professional growth.

My introduction to Anela came during a pivotal period in my life. As a young student at the United States Military Academy, her presence was synonymous with unwavering leadership and dedication. Over the years, she transitioned from being my supervisor and instructor to becoming a steadfast mentor who continues to inspire me today, over twenty years later.

It is with great admiration that I now have the privilege to introduce *Becoming All You Can Be: A Personal Growth Journey to Awakening, Transformation, and Wisdom*, authored by Anela Arcari. This book represents a culmination of her decades-long commitment to empowering others to reach their full potential. Drawing from her extensive military background and enriched by her experiences as a mentor and coach, Anela offers a comprehensive beginner's guide to personal growth and fulfillment.

Becoming All You Can Be is not merely a collection of motivational insights; it is a practical handbook designed to navigate life's challenges with resilience and clarity. Through poignant narratives and thought-provoking journal prompts, Anela encourages readers to embark on a journey of self-discovery. Her storytelling is as captivating and timeless as Aesop's fables—each tale, like her famous chicken curry story, carries profound lessons about perseverance and evolution. It underscores a universal truth: that it does not matter who you are, your circumstances, or background—Anela's stories, the lessons within them, and the enduring relevance of her wisdom transcend time, place, and people. Her approach combines insights gained from overcoming personal adversity with actionable strategies for achieving personal and professional success. This unique blend ensures that readers grasp the universal nature of her teachings, irrespective of individual circumstances or background.

Anela is not just a purveyor of wisdom, but a living example of the principles she espouses. Her actions align with her words; she walks the walk and talks the talk. She consistently emphasizes that everything we need to succeed is already within us, echoing the sentiment of Ralph Waldo Emerson's timeless quote, an all-time favorite of mine: "What lies behind us and what lies before us are tiny matters compared to what lies within us."

In conclusion, *Becoming All You Can Be: A Personal Growth Journey to Awakening, Transformation, and Wisdom* is more than a guidebook; it is a testament to the transformative power of courage, resilience, and self-discovery. Anela Arcari's compassionate voice and steadfast commitment to empowering others shines through every page, offering *you* a roadmap to unlock your true potential.

It is with immense gratitude and respect that I recommend this book to you. May it inspire and empower you on your journey of becoming all you can be.

Hugs and high fives,

Dr. CaS Facciponti
MAJ(R), US Army

INTRODUCTION

T hank you for choosing to read this book. Something in the title or on the back cover spoke to you. I thank you for listening to the urge to put this book in your hands or on your tablet. Since I know that everything happens *for* us, it is my deepest hope that you find the right nuggets for you on your path to becoming all you can be.

I struggled with how to best organize the stories in this book and ultimately decided to put them in chronological order. That turned out to be *the* gift. I wrote in my first published chapter in *Turning Point Moments*, "Only when we look back can we connect the dots that have brought us to our own light, to our destiny." I now realize these stories are the strongest examples of lessons I learned on my personal path to shining my light and becoming all I can be.

I grew up in an Army family, and I am proud of that beginning. So much of my early childhood shaped me into the person I am today. I am a proud Army Brat—a child of a service member who makes the military a career, resulting in a childhood spent in many places around the world on military assignments. My younger years played a role in my decision at age thirteen to join the military.

I was born in Hawaii while my father was in Vietnam. The name *Anela* is the Hawaiian name for angel. Just before my fourth birthday, we moved to Langdon, North Dakota, which was such a dramatic change in climate. Next, my father's career took us overseas to Camp Darby, Italy, Riyadh, Saudi Arabia, and Heidelberg, West Germany.

We lived ten minutes from the Leaning Tower of Pisa when I was in first grade. In second grade, I attended an international school in Riyadh and had the opportunity to walk through the opulent gold souks (bazaars). We then moved to Heidelberg for the next five years. I have always considered the Heidelberg castle *my castle* since I served as a flower girl in its chapel. To this day, my time in Heidelberg is the longest I've ever lived anywhere.

My number one hobby is traveling. I believe travel is one of the greatest gifts I received from being an Army brat. I have my parents and the Girl Scouts to thank for the joy that it brings me. Before I was in eighth grade, my family vacationed in some of the most famous places in Europe—Athens, Rome, Venice, Florence, Madrid, Barcelona, Mont-Saint-Michel, Normandy, Vienna, Salzburg, Zermatt, Luzern, Dublin, and Taormina. On our trip to Zermatt, I started my first travel journal.

Many of my adventures stemmed from being in the Girl Scouts. My troop, led by my mother, earned patches for every location we explored. We took weekend trips to

Paris, Munich, Frankfurt, West Berlin, Amsterdam, and Brussels. In Munich, we saw the solid gold funerary mask of the boy-king Tutankhamun. My troop also spent a week in London and a week in a chalet in Switzerland. In addition to taking in the crown jewels while in London, we went to see the musical *Annie*. I loved my European adventures, and each experience played a role in my becoming all I can be.

When I graduated from college and commissioned into the Army, *Be All You Can Be* was the Army motto. It came with a catchy tune that played during the commercials. The lyrics mentioned doing more before 9:00 a.m. than most people do all day. It was true; some days I did do more before 9:00 a.m. than some people did all day. That motto touched me deeply.

The motto accurately points to the fact that we each have a unique talent. When we leverage that talent, we can be the best version of ourselves. Imagine a world where we are all being the best we can be! I found it motivating and inclusive, and I was disappointed when, early in 2001, the Army adopted a new motto.

For many years, people suggested that I share stories from growing up and serving in the military. Taking that advice, I joined a writing group during COVID and began sharing some of my military experiences. The members told me I was *humanizing* the military. I had never heard that word before. The idea that I could help others see the human side of the military further encouraged my writing.

At the same time, I signed up for my first course with Christine Kloser, *The Sacred Container*. As part of my tuition, I received her *Get Your Book Done* course. I knew it was time to write my book. As I considered what the book might be about, it occurred to me that I've told many of my stories over and over. As I wondered why I repeated them, I discovered each one held a lesson that shaped me.

Being a lifelong seeker of personal growth, I learned from my spiritual mentor, Debra Poneman, that storytelling is a powerful way to teach. People remember stories. They help people connect to the message, and they can be more entertaining than a list of facts or lessons.

I wondered, *What if I could combine my love of journaling, storytelling, and the military into my first book to help others on their path to becoming all they can be?*

This book is that combination. It is a beginning. Life is a journey, not a destination. For me, *becoming* leads to *being*, and *being* leads to *be*. This is a collection of stories about the becoming part of my life journey.

It is not lost on me that now, after decades of talking about drafting this book, the Army has gone back to the motto, *Be All You Can Be*. If our purpose in life is to realize the talent that makes our heart sing, then the journey to discover that gift is about becoming all you can be.

If you bought or received this book, my guess is that you already journal or you have a desire to start journaling. This book is for you, wherever you are on your path. I hope by reading this book and engaging in the journal exercises, you will discover the stories of your life that have taught you your greatest lessons. Each story and its lesson are a part of you becoming all you can be and may further clarify the gift that the world is waiting for you to share.

To support your discovery of becoming all you can be, I've included questions at the end of each chapter and created a companion journal you can download *Becoming All You Can Be: A Companion Journal* (www. AnelaArcari.com) and use as you read this book. Or you can use your favorite journal to capture moments in your life that may point to your unique and wonderful gifts.

We all have stories and the lessons we learned from them. May you be inspired to inspire others by sharing yours.

Next: Despite my best efforts to ignore my true calling to write, my love of writing started at a young age when I began to journal. Chapter 1 shares the story of my first journal.

CHAPTER 1

TO JOURNAL OR NOT TO JOURNAL

In sixth grade, I received an assignment to read a powerful book. I had never heard of Anne Frank before reading her inspiring and heartfelt words. This young girl's diary conveyed the thoughts and feelings of a Jewish teenage girl while hiding to avoid persecution. Who does that? Keeps a journal under such trying times?

What fascinated me the most was the fact that when she wrote it, she had no idea that one day it would be found and published in seventy languages. It also became a movie and a play. I thought to myself: *How can one teenage girl have such an impact on the world?* My eyes were opened to the powerful impact one person could make, even a young girl like me. Eighty years later, her journal continues to inspire.

After reading the book, I began my first journal. Not because I thought someone would read it one day and be inspired (or maybe subconsciously that is what

I imagined), but I felt moved to write about my life, to reflect on things I struggled with—to vent and release.

I am not sure if I truly understood venting or releasing or why I felt compelled to begin journaling; I just knew I had to start writing. I believe now that I felt compelled because writing is a part of my calling. Writing is how I shine my light and how I add to the light of the world—through my storytelling.

Later in the year, my English teacher asked me to stay after class. Like most young students, I wondered what I had done wrong. As it turned out, he complemented me on my writing abilities and told me I could be a writer one day. He encouraged me to keep a journal and write in it every day. He said it would help me refine my writing style and improve my paragraph development, grammar, and punctuation.

I proudly explained that since finishing his assignment to read *The Diary of Anne Frank*, I was already journaling. I could see him light up as a big smile beamed across his face. I imagine every teacher lives for those moments when their student connects the dots of the coursework and furthers their own growth and understanding.

To this day, I still write in a journal, but not every day like I used to. I write not so much to vent but to reflect on events I perceive as happy or *good*, feeling like expansions, and on events that I perceive as sad or *bad*, feeling like contractions.

I also have several journals now. One is for gratitude, one is for recording small and big miracles, one is for my travels, one is for my book ideas, and one is for processing my sessions with my life and enneagram coaches. I decided to separate my journals because I found it easier to focus on one topic instead of searching through a single journal for the gratitude or travel section. However, I have clients who prefer to keep all their journal writing in one journal. There is no right way or wrong way; it is a personal preference.

If you are skeptical about journaling, great! Let me suggest a movie and a movement that might further demonstrate the power of journaling. If you haven't seen the movie *Freedom Writers*, I encourage you to watch it or look up the Freedom Writers Foundation.

The movie tells the story of one inner city teacher, Erin Gruwell, and her ingenious use of journaling to reach some of the toughest students who were labeled *unteachable*. The Foundation's website states, "Her students were particularly inspired by the writings of Anne Frank and Zlata Filipovic, and ultimately chose to put down their weapons and pick up their pen" (Freedom Writers Foundation). I am so enthusiastic about the power of journaling, a portion of the proceeds of the sale of this book will go to the Freedom Writers Foundation.

I encourage you to consider picking up a journal and giving it a try. To inspire you, here are the first questions to engage you in journaling, storytelling, and maybe teaching through your stories. You can download *Becoming All You Can Be: A Companion Journal* here: www.AnelaArcari.com

Journal Exercise

1. As a child, what did you dream of becoming?
2. What are the dreams you still hold?

Do you have concerns about writing down your feelings and thoughts? When I first started journaling, one of my fears was that someone would read my innermost thoughts and feelings. Eventually, the peace and joy that writing brought me outweighed any fear about someone reading my journal. If it was something I didn't want others to read, I created a code name or used an initial that only made sense to me.

Perhaps you think you don't have enough time. To that I ask: Are you willing to wake up five minutes early each day and start with a few minutes of writing? If journaling proves helpful to you, chances are you'll be willing to wake up ten minutes early, and then, before you know it, you will have created a habit that works for you and fits into your schedule.

CHAPTER 2

THE BEGINNING

When I was about eight years old, my family moved to Heidelberg, West Germany. We moved during the height of the Cold War, and the Berlin Wall stood as tall and as strong as ever. During those formative years, I experienced several scary events. I've included four of the most traumatic experiences as part of this chapter because they formed my belief that the world is unsafe. I had no idea I had experienced trauma at such a young age—I thought it was *normal*.

Our military community consisted of large four-story apartment buildings with twelve families residing in each building. Shortly after moving, I faced one of the most terrifying incidents of my young life.

Since it was pitch black outside, I assumed it was the middle of the night. I was sound asleep when out of nowhere came a male American voice over a loudspeaker.

Having never heard this commotion before, I jumped out of bed and went toward the window.

We lived on the third floor, so I had a bird's-eye view of a military police vehicle driving slowly down the road between two tall apartment buildings filled with American military families. The vehicle's lights were flashing. There were no sirens, but the occupants constantly broadcasted a string of words and numbers that held no meaning for me.

As they inched by, I watched light after light go on in each apartment. I am sure the light in my parents' bedroom also turned on, but I was so scared and mesmerized by what I was watching, I don't remember hearing our front door open or close. I distinctly remember watching one soldier after another (someone's dad) come out of their apartment building—wearing their combat uniform—and walk down the street towards the main headquarters.

It is important to note that my father seldom wore his combat uniform. He worked in a large headquarters in which they wore their Army Class A green uniform (with coat and tie) every day. To see all these soldiers walking out of their homes in combat uniforms and combat gear filled me with such uncertainty. However, I remained glued to the glass, frozen in fear and morbid curiosity. I could not pull myself away from the window although what I was witnessing terrified me. I felt like my heart would burst out of my chest any second as it seemed to beat a thousand beats per minute.

Then I saw my father walk out of our building and down the street, joining all the other soldiers going off to war—that is what it looked like to me. Complete dread and bewilderment washed over me. I found myself wondering if I would ever see my dad again. I had no idea what was going on or what it all meant. I felt confused, scared, lost, and abandoned. I stayed until I couldn't see any of them any longer as if continuing to watch would somehow bring them all home again.

I didn't know it was only a drill; I only wondered when or if I would see my dad again.

We did eventually learn that it was drill and that there might come a day when it was not a drill. If that day came, Dad would walk into work prepared to go to war, and my mother, sister, and I would be sent back to the United States, not knowing when or if we would see him again. Those drills continued for the five years we lived in Germany and caused me to wake up out of a sound sleep with my heart pounding, wondering if this was the time the flashing lights and loudspeaker announcements were not a drill. I came to accept this abnormal routine as *normal* and chalked it up to being a part of a military family.

After surviving the rude awakening go-to-war calls, I soon found out it was not safe to go to school either. Another regular and terrifying event was a bomb threat called into our elementary school or the connected high school. When a call happened, the administration had to treat it as real. So, we evacuated the school as if it were a fire drill and walked across the street into the closest four-story American apartment building. Once inside the building, we would either gather in the basement, or we would fill up the stairwell from the basement to the attic. We would sit and chat with our friends while bomb dogs would meticulously search every room of both schools. It seemed like hours before we were able to go back into the classroom. At that point, we were so riled up, nervous, and tired, it was difficult to continue any meaningful schoolwork.

While these bomb threats continued and actual car bombs were detonated in the city where we lived, thankfully, no senior US government officials were harmed. Simultaneously, the Iranian hostage crisis also kicked off. Within days, I heard stories of a man my parents knew who talked to the American diplomats in the embassy the day the Iranians stormed the compound. He supposedly instructed them how to destroy sensitive documents and stayed on the phone with them until the line went dead. I do not know if that happened, but when I heard the story, all I could think about was what it might be like to be talking with those desperate embassy employees right up until their last moment of freedom.

Like many Americans, I watched every day, I prayed, and I eventually celebrated when the hostages were finally released after fourteen months of captivity. It was an excessively big deal in West Germany because they stopped in Wiesbaden (about sixty miles from

Heidelberg), to be evaluated by American doctors. Adjacent to the hospital was a residential building called the Amelia Earhart Hotel. The former hostages and some of their family members stayed there while they underwent evaluation and received treatments.

Several years later, I received an assignment in Wiesbaden and went to work on the ninth floor in what is now an office building known as the Amelia Earhart Building. Every day on the way to my office, I passed by a plaque on the wall commemorating that historic event and their stay in that building when they were freed after 444 days of captivity. Reading the plaque each day inspired me and reminded me to always remain hopeful.

The most significant trauma I experienced involved a kidnapping that took place in Italy. One day, men posing as maintenance crew members entered an American general's home and took him hostage. While we weren't living in Italy at the time, we had lived there a few years before this incident, and the boldness and simplicity of the attack affectedly me deeply. I felt connected to this man in a way I can't explain, and it touched me as if it were my dad who was kidnapped.

On some level, I thought if it could happen to a general officer, it could happen to my dad or any number of other soldiers living in Europe at the time. Every day, I watched the news or listened to the radio to learn the fate of this man. I prayed for him and his family and waited to learn more about where he was and how his captors treated him. I feared they would kill him, and I anxiously waited for word of his release.

One night after he was released, I had the most vivid dream of my young life. In this dream, my family was in a building with the general and his wife. We were getting ready to attend a welcome home ceremony. A security team took us up several flights of stairs to a waiting room before heading to the large auditorium filled with people celebrating the general's release. However, when we got into the waiting room, the security detail told us that as we were climbing the stairs, they had discovered two bombs.

I thought: *Why did they wait to tell us at the top of the stairs?*

They directed us to quickly go back down the stairs. My mother and I were the lasts ones to leave the waiting room, and surprisingly, on every landing of the staircase was an unmade bed. I grew up in a home in which beds were made every single day. So, I was not surprised when my mother directed me to make every bed before going down to the next floor. I knew we had to hurry, so I wasn't making the beds, but they blocked our path. So, we had to climb over each bed before going down to the next level of stairs.

It was the strangest dream. As a result, my mother and I didn't escape the building before the bombs went off. I saw a big flash of light as the bombs exploded and immediately knew my mother and I didn't make it.

This was the first time I died in my dreams. It jolted me in a way I find hard to put into words. I did not wake up at that moment; the dream continued. The big auditorium filled with people celebrating the general's release became a memorial service for my mom and me. In the dream, I was floating above the stage as if my spirit were up in the rafters. I was looking down at my father, sister, the general, and his wife as they participated in my memorial. Then I woke up.

Despite knowing the general was rescued and came home safely, I never really got over that terrifying dream or the feeling of dying in the bomb blast.

While I am not sure these stories are *the* beginning, they are early traumatic childhood memories that significantly shaped my life in ways I didn't begin to understand until well into adulthood. The early morning alerts, bomb threats, hostage crisis, and the terrorist attacks all became routine, expected, and a part of my everyday life, so I was fifty before I considered their actual impact. I thought trauma was caused by physical or emotional abuse, so I believed I had a normal childhood that did not include any trauma. However, each of these events was jarring and left a huge imprint on my body, mind, psyche, and soul in ways I am still uncovering, unpacking, and processing.

Today, children face similar traumas preparing for and living through an active shooter at school—sadly almost daily. Trauma comes in all shapes and sizes. It does not discriminate. I grew up in a happy, well-adjusted family. And yet, events like this did scar me and shape my sense of security and safety—or lack of it—well into my adulthood. Even though my traumas might be less egregious than other traumas, their comparative results don't make them any less significant in the ways they affected me and my life.

Don't compare your childhood experiences to others. Additionally, no matter your experiences or traumas, do not allow anyone to diminish or define their impact on your life.

We all have a choice in how to acknowledge and traverse traumas' effects. That journey of navigating life and choosing victory over victimhood matters and gives us hope.

You are the sum of your experiences and how you decide each next step leads to becoming all you can be.

Journal Exercise

The most important decision we make is whether we believe we live in a friendly or hostile universe.
—attributed to Albert Einstein

1. Think about this quote and your earliest memories. Did you believe you lived in a friendly or hostile universe?
2. Up until now, how has that belief shaped your experience of life?
3. Do you feel it is possible to shift that belief?

CHAPTER 3

FREEDOM IS PRECIOUS

It is two o'clock in the morning, and I am nine years old on an overnight train doing exactly what I was instructed not to do—peeking through the drawn curtain. I am doing it as surreptitiously as I possibly can. My curiosity is far greater than my fear of getting caught; I cannot help myself. I am a part of a Girl Scout troop, and we are on the Duty Train to West Berlin, but it feels like a James Bond movie. What could be so interesting that I would stay up all night and risk my life, or at the very least, cause an international incident?

The Duty Train, you ask? What is that? West Berlin?

The Duty Train was a US military train that traveled from Frankfurt, West Germany, to West Berlin, East Germany, in the late 70s and early 80s. Americans traveled on it to West Berlin for business and vacation. This sanctioned train left Frankfurt in the late afternoon so that everyone on the train would be sleeping while they traveled through East Germany. When they woke up, they were in West Berlin.

My brave mother was my Girl Scout leader, and she agreed—with the help of my father and older sister—to take our Girl Scout troop to West Berlin so that we could earn the *West Berlin patch*. This patch was granted to Girl Scouts who traveled to the city, explored its famous sights, and authored a report about the experience at the end of the adventure.

The military police who accompanied us on the Duty Train read strict rules to all the passengers before boarding the train. Among the rules, we were to draw our curtains closed and not open them until we arrived in West Berlin. They told us the train would stop during the night while passing through East Germany, but looking out the window when the train stopped was forbidden.

This restriction was for our own safety and was one of many agreements the US military made with the East German government that allowed the train to pass through their country without incident. Their firm tone left no doubt that we were to follow all instructions if we wanted to remain safe during the night. Since I trusted my mom and dad, I knew we would be okay, but I also felt nervous to be traveling through *enemy* territory.

Each compartment had six beds, and I requested one of the highest bunks, closest to the ceiling. I didn't plan to stay up all night; it just happened at this slumber party with five of my girlfriends. Then, as briefed, the train began stopping along the way. I realized I could pull back on the pleat at the very top of the curtain and peer down to see what was happening.

I believe the first stop was at the border between West Germany and East Germany. What I saw completely shocked me. I don't know what I expected, but I saw three East German soldiers who looked like young teenagers, fourteen or fifteen years old. Two were carrying large semi-automatic weapons ready to fire, if needed. The third soldier had his weapon slung across his back as he diligently searched the undercarriage using a large round mirror. Seeing their youth, their weapons drawn, and the mirror sweeping under our rail car made the journey scarier. I questioned: *What am I doing here?* I knew I wasn't supposed to be looking, and yet, once again, I could not pull myself away from the window. I remained frozen and silent in fear.

As the train pulled out of that checkpoint, I noticed that our railroad tracks were confined by a chain link fence on both sides. At that moment, I understood that the fence was there to prevent anyone from trying to escape to freedom. That realization set the tone for the entire trip, and looking back, it also played a considerable role on my path to become a protector of America's precious freedom. I appreciated for the very first time how very lucky I was to be an American, to be free!

Later that day, I climbed up many steps to a platform that brought me to the top of the Berlin Wall, and I looked over it into East Berlin. I saw more young soldiers staring back at me with their weapons pointed in my direction.

I remember thinking that every American should be required to stand at that wall and see what it looks like to not be free. Despite America's imperfections, I was so grateful to be a citizen of the United States, and I wanted to be a part of protecting it.

During that first trip to West Berlin, I bought a large poster of a building that became a part of the very first wall in East Berlin. Before they built the tall concrete wall, they just bricked up the windows of the buildings that were now on the *wrong* side of a line. At the very top of the poster was one word, WHY? That poster hung on my wall until I went to college. I looked at it every day and asked myself; *Why?* I never imagined the wall would come down. Then during my sophomore year in college, the *impossible* happened—the wall was torn down. It was such a joyous occasion to watch unfold, and the memory reminds me today that anything is *possible*.

Freedom is precious! Growing up in a military family taught me firsthand what it truly means to be free and gave me a deep appreciation for the many freedoms I enjoy.

As an adult, my concept of freedom includes the following considerations:

- *Am I free to be my most authentic self?*
- *Am I free to shine my light and be the best version of me?*

Journal Exercise

1. Are you free to be you?
2. Is there anything that holds you back from being you?
3. How might appreciating the freedoms you enjoy help you?

CHAPTER 4

COPING SKILL: BAD NEWS FIRST

When I was twelve years old, I had the amazing opportunity to attend a Girl Scout camp in Germany. It was called Camp Lachenwald or Camp Laughing Woods. It was the first overnight camp my parents allowed me to attend. I felt so grown up as we shopped for the packing list items. I was going away for two weeks, several hours from home.

In the weeks leading up to my departure, our beloved dog, Mocha, was beginning to lose the use of her back two legs. We got Mocha when I was four years old. We were living in North Dakota at the time, and she was my first family pet. I wanted so badly to name her *Princess*. I didn't understand the *rules* of naming a family pet: it had to fit the dog and make sense. Her name came from her coloring. She was a dark brown on top and a light brown on the bottom, thus together she was Mocha. Once it was explained to me, it made sense to me, but I was still disappointed that I didn't get to name her.

Mocha was a mix of cocker spaniel, dachshund, and poodle. We called her a CockaDachaPoo. She had the nose and face of a cocker spaniel, the long back and short legs of a dachshund, and the curly hair of a poodle. She was adorable as a puppy and a bit eccentric looking as she grew older. One of my more vivid memories was when she gave birth to her puppies. Seeing them being born, watching her clean them up right after their birth, seeing how they navigated before their eyes opened, watching them nurse, and eventually finding new homes for all of them was a unique experience.

She moved with us from North Dakota, to Italy, Saudi Arabia, and West Germany. In Germany, we lived on the third floor, so she climbed many stairs each time we took her out for a walk. What we didn't know was that the long back of a dachshund is fragile and not built to climb that many stairs. Had we known, we would have carried her up and down all those stairs.

As her mobility began to deteriorate, Mom brought her to a German veterinarian. We discovered they were forward-thinking for the early 80s, recommending acupuncture for her back as a possible treatment. While unorthodox in our mind, we were hopeful. I even imagined we could rig up some wheels for her hind legs to help with her mobility.

As I got ready to leave for camp, she seemed okay, but there was a part of me that knew to say goodbye to her before I left. The day I left for camp, I got down on the floor and held her close, wishing her well and wondering if I would see her again. I wished her comfort and asked her to feel better, to live.

Mom, Dad, and my sister dropped me off at camp. I don't know that I understood that going off to camp by myself was a rite of passage. I was excited and nervous; they were excited and nervous too. What if I became so homesick I wanted to come home? I don't remember asking that question, but I know it went through my head.

It turned out to be an amazing experience filled with so much fun and laughter. The name of the camp was perfect because every day, my tent mates and I laughed so hard our sides hurt.

The two weeks were one great adventure, and while I was very happy to see my family, I was also very sad to leave camp. I had a great time every day, made so many new friends, and couldn't wait to come back the next year to be reunited with my newfound friends.

Shortly after we got in the car, my sister said she had good news and bad news and asked which one I wanted first. Without really thinking much about it, I blurted out to share bad news first. She told me with tears in her eyes that while I was gone, Mocha stopped eating and that they put her to sleep. Although I was not surprised by the news, I, too, began to cry. Even though I knew that one day she would die, it was sad to lose a member of the family. Of course, knowing that reality and experiencing the loss are two very different things.

Then I remembered my sister still had good news to share with me.

I anxiously asked, "So what's the good news?"

She showed me a small diamond ring on her left ring finger and explained it was a promise ring, not an engagement ring. I didn't really understand the difference, and I didn't care. I was so happy that I started to cry happy tears. My big sister was getting married. Not right away. She would go to college and graduate first. I didn't care when she was getting engaged or married; I simply knew she was getting married, and that was exciting, happy news.

I was still sad about going home to an apartment without Mocha, and each time I thought about Mocha, I remembered the excitement of my sister getting married. I don't know if I truly appreciated the sheer wisdom of asking for the bad news first, but it became a mantra of mine. I always picked bad news first anytime anyone told me they had good news and bad news. I taught it to others every chance I got and always received feedback that it was helpful advice.

The next time someone offers good news and bad news, maybe start with the bad news first. While the good news does not make the bad news go away, it certainly lessens the sting of bad news and is the perfect reminder of the importance of contrast. We can't fully appreciate the sun without the rain, the light without the dark, and the joy without the sorrow. It is all a part of life, and one informs the other. Each will pass. None are permanent.

Journal Exercise

1. How have you come to appreciate or not appreciate contrast in your life?
2. Does one (rain, dark, sorrow) help understand or deal with the other (sun, light, joy)?

CHAPTER 5

GUARDED: BEING CALLED A NAZI

When my father retired from the military after nearly twenty-three years, we were still living in Heidelberg, West Germany. My parents decided to move back to Connecticut, since that is where they were born and raised and most of our extended family called home. They had never owned a home in Connecticut, and while staying at my Godmother's summer cottage the year before, they had decided to buy a year-round home in the same town.

It was a summer community with a population of 10,000 during the winter, expanding to 30,000 in the summer. We arrived in our new house just weeks before I started eighth grade. When we moved to Connecticut, I had lived outside the United States for seven years. My dad was stationed in Italy for one year, Saudi Arabia for one year, and West Germany for five years. To say that I felt like a foreigner in my own country would be an understatement, but I didn't know I felt that way until I went to school. I was so naive; I did not realize I was *different*.

You may have heard the saying that kids can be so cruel. I didn't appreciate that until I moved back to the United States. On the bus to school on my first day, I sat near a fellow eighth grader, Martha, who recognized I was new. I didn't realize at that point that everyone else on the bus had been going to school together since kindergarten. Having grown up in a military family, the concept of going to school in the same town from kindergarten through twelfth grade was definitely a strange concept.

My newfound *friend*, Martha, proceeded to ask several questions about me and my background. Not knowing any better, I told her everything on the way to school. Much to my surprise, by the end of the day, the entire school—which consisted of all the seventh and eighth graders—knew my whole life story.

Besides the fact that I was the new girl, I quickly realized that clothes were important. When living overseas in a military community, there are limited shopping options—either the Post Exchange (PX) for clothes or from the local economy. There was no Amazon, so my mom bought the clothes that the Post Exchange carried, and back then, they did not carry Guess jeans or Izod shirts.

On top of everything else that already set me apart, I later found out that I dressed *funny*. I didn't appreciate fashion and, even after I discovered it, really couldn't be bothered driving myself crazy buying the right clothes to fit in. However, as a teenager, I wanted to fit in, so I begged my mom to buy certain pieces of clothing to look the way others looked. She was not about to spend money on any clothes with expensive labels. I may have managed to look the part, but I was still an outcast from the perspective that my labels weren't designer by any stretch of the imagination.

Those first few weeks were rough. I did eventually find a group of friends to eat lunch with, who happened to be the self-proclaimed *misfits*. We did not really fit into any of the other groups. We were not athletes. We were not the popular kids, but some of us were in the marching band. It was a small group of girls who celebrated being different, and they welcomed me with open arms.

I was introduced to the group by a student who was in my Industrial Arts class. I am so happy Chris walked up to me and had the courage to befriend the *foreigner*. We are still friends today. In fact, we refer to each other as BFFs—Best Friends Forever. Many years later, I asked Chris why she approached me in class, and she said it was because I was so different, and she found that interesting.

If I had to go through all the awkwardness of being an outcast to meet her, it was worth it. We both went on to serve in the military, and she continues to serve today, as a one-star general. I am extremely grateful to her and proud to call her my BFF.

After covering World War II in class one day, a fellow classmate who rode my bus to school thought that it would be funny to call me a Nazi. Gunner, like everyone else on the bus, knew I'd recently moved to Connecticut from West Germany. I am sure he was making a connection between what we were studying in history and a fact that he knew about me in his mind. I am also sure—based on the way Gunner and the rest of the bus laughed—that he called me the name to get a reaction from me and all our classmates on the bus.

I didn't say or do anything, even though I felt extremely embarrassed and deeply hurt. Gunner could not have picked a more damaging word to call me. I have told this story many times and said he could have called me a swear word and it wouldn't have hurt me as profoundly as calling me a Nazi. I didn't cry or even tell anyone in my family about what happened; I just took the pain and absorbed it into my body.

I would be thirty years old before I realized the profound impact that one word had on me, my psyche, my self-esteem, my sense of self. I was attending a retreat, and we did an exercise that led us through different times in our life. Based on the memory that surfaced, we answered a few questions and determined the character trait we decided to take on because of that experience. As if a light switch was flipped on, I discovered that, in that moment, I took on the trait of being *guarded*. I decided to never give anyone enough information to use against me.

As soon as I made that connection, I felt a huge weight lift off my heart area; I physically felt lighter. Making this discovery helped me release all the false beliefs I took on the day I was called a Nazi.

The next day, a co-worker asked me about the experience. I shared the entire story about being called a Nazi and the trait that I took on.

She said, "If I were to pick one word to describe you, it has always been *guarded* from the first day I met you."

Our conversation was further proof that I had uncovered something big. I was peeling that layer off, allowing me to drop that characteristic. I realize now that it allowed a bit more of my authentic self and light to shine through.

That is not to say that I am not sometimes still guarded—I am. I am also much better at recognizing that being guarded is a way I create separation and distance. Once I am aware, I can make the decision if I need to remain guarded because the situation calls for it or if it is safe for me to be open and vulnerable. With very few exceptions, I now choose to be open and vulnerable. Being called a Nazi provided me a valuable lesson and played a role in my becoming all I can be.

Journal Exercise

1. Is there a time in your life when someone labeled you?
2. What characteristic did you decide or choose to take on?
3. How is that trait serving you?
4. Is it a trait you wish to continue to carry? You may find it is time to let it go.

CHAPTER 6

SINK OR SWIM: HOW I LEARNED TO COOK

One day when I was in eighth grade, my mom said out of the blue, "Did I tell you that dinner is on you tonight?"

Flabbergasted, I said, "No!"

She said, "Yes, it is."

I really thought she was kidding at first, but quickly realized she was not joking. I attempted to protest, "But I've never made a whole meal before."

She retorted, "You know your way around the kitchen. You can do this." Followed with, "What would you like to make?"

I remember quickly trying to think of something easy to make because the idea of trying to orchestrate the timing of a main dish, vegetables, salad, and warm bread was way too overwhelming for a mainly sous-chef and dishwasher. *How does one time everything so that it all goes on the dining room table at the same time and is still warm?* That type of organizing, planning, and execution was beyond my comprehension. Then it hit me. I needed something easy that all cooked in one pan—like soup or a taco salad—and something I had both the ingredients and recipe for.

What turned out to be the hard part? A simple recipe. Most of the delicious meals Mom makes are stored in her head, ones she learned from her mother when she was growing up. If I was going to be on my own with no help from her, I required instructions.

After several tries, I thought of a dish that required one pan, some rice, and some condiments. I felt confident with her rice cooker; I could manage her chicken curry recipe.

Hesitantly, I asked, "Do you have an actual recipe for the chicken curry?"

Much to my surprise, she said, "As a matter of fact I do. It is in one of my favorite cookbooks called *Meals with a Foreign Flair.*" (I found out this is a thin *Better Homes and Gardens* hardbound cookbook.)

I let out a huge sigh of relief as she went to find the cookbook and made sure we had all the ingredients. I was still anxious but happy when she handed me the book and confirmed we had all the ingredients.

As if things couldn't get any worse for this fourteen-year-old, my mother then announced she was leaving the house.

"What? You are leaving?" I said.

She had to be kidding, right? Oh no, she wasn't kidding. She had some errands to run and would be back in time for dinner, around the same time Dad was expected home.

"But what if I need some help, or have a problem?" I asked.

"Anela, we just walked through everything, and you have everything you need. You got this," she reassuringly said as she grabbed her purse and the car keys. Then she walked out the door.

I couldn't believe it! When I, this vulnerable and slightly dramatic teenager needed her mom the most, she walked out the door and drove away. Talk about a sink-or-swim moment in my life. I stood there in shock for a few minutes and quickly realized if I didn't get started, we weren't eating dinner that night.

Looking at the recipe, I thought the first part would be easy as it contained my familiar sous-chef duties.

Then a flood of thoughts ran through my mind: *How long did she say the rice cooks in the rice cooker? Do I need to start that now? If dinner needs to be ready at 5:30, and the rice takes 30 minutes, I will start the rice at 4:50 to give myself a buffer. Okay, I got this. No worries! Back to the cutting board.*

But as I looked at the recipe, I saw it called for two cups of cooked chicken. The chicken I had wasn't cooked. I realized I needed another pan for that, and the recipe did not give instructions for cooking the chicken.

Great, something else I need to figure out and factor into the timing of the meal.

I stuck with what I was most comfortable with, chopping—that was easy and brought me a level of comfort, helping me calm down. I followed the order of the recipe. First I chopped the apple, then the onion (I discovered onions made me cry), then the celery, and finally the mushrooms.

With that prep work done, I cut up the chicken. I knew enough about cooking that I knew I needed to put something in the pan before I cooked the chicken, so I chose a little butter. Much to my surprise, it cooked up nicely and quite easily. I removed the chicken from the pan and realized I could use the same pan to make the rest of the meal. I was so proud of myself for not using every single pan in the house for one meal.

With all the prep work completed, I was delighted at how easy the rest of the meal came together. And it was all in one pan (minus the rice)! I started the rice cooker, so by the time Mom returned, I had set the table and was waiting for the rice to finish.

Then she threw a wrench. "What about the condiments?"

You would have thought she said something that would ruin the whole meal by my reaction. In rapid fire succession, I asked, "What about the condiments? Where are they? What do I do with them?"

As I went through my mini panic attack, she got out four bowls and directed me to the chutney, coconut, peanuts, and raisins.

Somewhere in the chaos, Dad came home, and as soon as the condiments were on the table, we sat down for dinner. I was so incredibly proud of myself; everything was still hot, and I couldn't wait to tell my dad that I had made the entire meal myself. To this day, much to my mother's chagrin, he always asks me to make him chicken curry because he swears mine is better.

For me, this experience that started out as sheer dread launched my absolute love of cooking. I truly enjoy everything about it, but most of all, I love to share the finished creations with people I love. There is such joy and magic in pulling a bunch of disparate ingredients together to make a mouthwatering masterpiece. Seeing the fruits of my labor from start to finish brings such a sense of accomplishment and great peace, especially when everything around me seems to be so out of control. I love, love, love cooking and baking—seeing the joy in loved ones' faces and hearing their satisfied: *mmm, that's good.*

I am forever grateful for that fateful day in eighth grade when Mom asked me, "Did I tell you dinner is on you tonight?"

When forced to sink or swim, I learned to not give in to resistance. I initially resisted the idea that I could cook a meal by myself. By facing that resistance, not letting it stop me, I discovered my fear wasn't as big as I made it in my mind. I didn't believe I could cook, and without that sink-or-swim moment, I could have decided not to try. By going with the opportunity, this experience showed me what is possible when I flow *with* instead of fighting *against* the current. Now when I feel resistance, I remember my first meal experience and decide to lean in and go with the opportunity.

Journal Exercise

1. Is there a time you resisted trying something new?
2. What did you learn from that experience? Could you use what you learned to teach others something new?

Chicken Curry Recipe
1 tablespoon curry powder
1 cup diced pared apple
1 tablespoon butter
1 onion, minced
1 cup sliced celery
½ cup sliced mushrooms
½ cup condensed beef broth
1 cup light cream
1 cup milk
2 tablespoons cornstarch
2 tablespoons cold water
2 cups diced cooked chicken
1 teaspoon salt

Sauté curry powder and apple in butter until apple is soft; stir in vegetables; mix thoroughly. Add beef broth; bring to boil, then stir in cream and milk; bring just to boil again.

Combine cornstarch and cold water; add and cook, stirring constantly, until mixture thickens. Stir in remaining ingredients. Serve with rice.

Offer condiments: chutney, salted peanuts, coconut, raisins.

Makes 5 or 6 servings.

(Better Homes and Gardens 1963)

P.S. The reason Dad likes my chicken curry better? I use two cups of heavy cream instead of one cup of light cream and one cup of milk.

Better Homes & Gardens

Meals with a FOREIGN FLAIR

100 recipes
from 18 countries! Main
dishes, desserts, breads,
salads–prize souvenirs
from around the world!

Chicken Curry

1 tablespoon curry powder
1 cup diced pared apple
1 tablespoon butter
1 onion, minced
1 cup sliced celery
½ cup sliced mushrooms
¾ cup condensed beef broth
1 cup light cream
1 cup milk
2 tablespoons cornstarch
2 tablespoons cold water
2 cups diced cooked chicken
1 teaspoon monosodium glutamate
1 teaspoon salt

Saute curry powder and apple in butter until apple is soft; stir in vegetables; mix thoroughly. Add beef broth; bring to boil, then stir in cream and milk; bring just to boil again.

Combine cornstarch and cold water; add, and cook, stirring constantly, till mixture thickens. Stir in remaining ingredients. To match picture, page 29, trim with preserved kumquats and parsley. Serve with rice. Offer condiments—watermelon pickles, chutney, salted peanuts, coconut, raisins. Makes 5 or 6 servings.

CHAPTER 7

NEVER SAY NEVER

Speaking of not resisting—the first time I heard about Mercy High School (before we moved to Connecticut) and learned that it was an all-girls Catholic high school where they wore plaid polyester skirts, I thought: *That does not sound the least bit like fun.* I made up my mind right then, having never seen the school, that I would never go to Mercy.

What are those sayings: *Never say never* or *Make a plan and God laughs at you*?

Due to the lack of a warm welcome, eighth grade turned into a pivotal and critical year that shaped my future in significant and meaningful ways. It wasn't long before discussions with lunchmates began to include where we would go to high school. There were two main choices: the public high school in town or—you guessed it—the private, all-girls Catholic high school, Mercy.

I remained adamant that I would not attend *that* school. Halfway through the school year, Mercy and its counterpart—the all-boys school, Xavier—announced the dates for their entrance exams. Seriously, one had to take an entrance exam for the privilege of wearing a uniform to school? *No thank you.* No resistance there!

As the dates for the entrance exams drew closer, my mom asked me each week if I wanted to sit for the exams. Each time she asked, I responded emphatically, *no*. Then, right at the deadline to register for the exams, she presented logic against which I could not argue.

She knew that some of my friends already planned to attend Mercy, so she said, "What if, at the end of the year, you decided you wanted to join them at Mercy? If you don't take the exams now, you will not have the option to pick Mercy later."

That made too much sense and I had no rebuttal. So begrudgingly, I agreed to take the exam.

The day of the exams, it was snowy and a bit icy, and I had a cold. We lived a good thirty minutes away, and my incredible dad was ready to brave the weather to get me there on time. I was such an insolent child that day. I had a disdainful, hands-on-hips, *you can't make me* attitude. I was rude and mean to my mother who—I realize looking back—only wanted the absolute best for me.

She gave me a small pouch with everything I needed: two number two sharpened pencils, a three-by-five card with all the pertinent information I would need to fill out the test paperwork, and a package of tissues because she knew I wasn't feeling well. I flippantly grabbed it from her as I walked out the door. I am ashamed of how disrespectful I was to her that morning.

On the way to the school, I decided that since I didn't feel well, I would guess on any question that required me to add, subtract, multiply, or divide. A mere two fifths of the test. That stubborn, Taurus teenager stuck to her foolish, resistant, self-sabotaging decision. I still have a copy of those test results. It looks like a big W as the three high scores were the reading and comprehension parts of the test and the two low scores were the math parts of the test.

A few months later, Mercy held an open house, and once again, I begrudgingly agreed to attend with my parents. The open house started in the auditorium with an overview of the school and many of its academic and extracurricular activities. It was clear from the presentations that Mercy had a great reputation and excellent academic program—98 percent of its students went on to higher education upon graduation. That was a significant statistic that, even in my rebellious state, I knew was important.

After the presentations in the auditorium, we were broken into small groups and assigned to a senior and a junior, who took us on a tour of the pristine and immaculately clean school. The hallways were carpeted and spotless. What high school has carpets in the hallways, let alone spotless ones with not one patch of gum or dirt?

While I am sure they took us to every part of the school, what impressed me—and ultimately convinced me to attend—was the tour guides' genuine and pure love of their school. Both young ladies oozed complete joy and unwavering loyalty and admiration for Mercy High School. It was undeniable and contagious.

Not only was I convinced this was the school for me, but I also knew that one day I would volunteer to take future prospective students on this same tour. I also knew, without any doubt, I would ooze the same level of enthusiasm and love of Mercy that these two women of Mercy shared with me.

And the purely defiant teenager kept that decision a complete secret for several years. With my less than stellar test scores, I applied to Mercy as far as my parents knew, simply to appease them. Secretly, I worried that my test scores would keep me from my new dream to attend Mercy.

One day after school, I checked the mail and saw an envelope addressed to my parents from Mercy High School. I was certain it was the announcement about my acceptance or rejection. I had no idea what time my parents would be home, and I didn't want to wait another minute to know the outcome.

I had the brilliant idea to steam the envelope open—exactly how I'd seen it done on TV or in the movies. That way I could, or so I thought, open the envelope without anyone knowing, read the results, and close the envelope. No harm, no fowl.

Have you ever tried to steam open an envelope? There is probably a YouTube video now that shows the proper way to use steam to open an envelope undetected. Of course, this was long before *how-to* videos. I assure you, what I did was not the way to open an envelope using steam.

I boiled a small pan of water and held the envelope over the steam, which softened the entire seal and also wrinkled the whole backside of the envelope. When that happened, I panicked because I realized there would be no way to cover up the fact that I had tampered with the envelope. How was I going to explain opening my parents' mail? With a now soggy envelope, I carefully tried to open it just along the sealed edge but ended up tearing bits and pieces all along the seal. There was no technique I could use to put the envelope back together in any way that would look unopened.

What was I going to do?

At the same time, I was also very anxious to read the letter. What if I didn't get accepted? How would I handle the rejection now that I had my heart set on attending Mercy? In that moment, the destroyed envelope and fear of rejection were all mixed together, and I had to know.

I pulled the completely soggy letter out of the now tattered envelope and carefully opened it. Much to my elation, and a bit to my surprise given my test scores, I was accepted. Inside, I was doing a happy dance. Outside, I was extremely worried about how much trouble I was in for tampering with the mail. I did put the letter back in the envelope and attempted to close it, but there was no way to hide the mess I had made steaming the envelope.

As I paced around the house trying to come up with a viable solution, the phone rang. It was Mom calling from work to see how my afternoon was going. I blurted out as nonchalantly and indifferently as I could that there was a letter from Mercy High School. Much to my surprise and complete relief, she invited me to open the letter and read it.

With the greatest amount of nonchalance I could muster, I said, "Oh, I got in."

She proceeded to hoot and congratulate me over the phone, and inside, I continued my happy dance. She was incredibly excited for me, and I could now throw away the envelope with no one being any the wiser.

My resistant *I do not want to go to Mercy* spirit did not stop there. I continued the charade for several more months. My sister was attending college in Connecticut at that time, and it was agreed that I would spend my spring break with her. Before I left, Mom told me it was time to send in the deposit for Mercy and that I was not to leave on spring break until I told her my final decision. To seal the deal, she brought out what I called the *big guns*, my dad. The fact that Mom felt the need to bring him in is further proof of how well I kept the secret that I had already made up my mind to attend.

Dad has always been a man of very few words, and when he does speak, he leaves no doubt about his message. Those few words are powerful and often words to live by. At this point in my young life, she had already used this tactic one other time to much success. That conversation involved their reasons for not allowing me to attend a formal, prom-like dance in seventh grade. In that instance, his logic was sound, and I left the conversation feeling much better about their *no*.

Since the heart-to-heart conversations with Dad were rare, I knew this was especially important to both of them. While I don't remember all the parts of the conversation, I do remember the main point. While he had attended public high school and married his high school sweetheart, he had friends and my mom's sister who had attended private high school.

He spoke highly of public school and reminded me that it prepared him for college and life. Then he explained that by attending a private school, and in this case a Catholic school, I would experience something extra, something special that was intangible. Even though he couldn't easily put it into words, I felt that he knew what he was talking about and that if I went to Mercy, I would graduate with this special ingredient. I left that conversation wholeheartedly knowing I was making the absolute best decision for myself.

I did go off to my sister's college without giving Mom my definitive answer—rebel witch with a capital *B* to the end! In those days, there was one pay phone on each floor by the elevators. When it rang, you hoped someone in a room close to the elevators would answer it. Luckily for me, someone did, and they walked to the end of the hall to let my sister know she had a phone call. She walked down to the elevators and found out the call was for me, so she walked back to her room to get me.

I knew who was on the phone, and my sister shared that Mom was not too happy. I walked down to the phone, dreading the conversation. Rightfully so, Mom was disappointed in me, and no child ever wants to disappoint their parents. To the bitter end, and with all the apathy and disinterest I could infuse into my voice, I said something like, "Yeah, I guess I'll go.

That resulted in the whole, "Do not do this for me, and we cannot get this refund back, so you better be sure this is what you want" conversation. With one final roll of my eyes, I told her again with a *whatever* tone that I wanted to go and wouldn't change my mind. We hung up, and I walked to my sister's room doing my happy dance inside and out.

I was an adult long before I ever came clean about when I made my decision to go and my attempt to steam open the envelope. It remains a funny story we share within the family. I realize now how incredibly lucky I am to have such loving parents who put up with all that teenage angst and resistance. More importantly, I realize how blessed I am that they had the financial means to send me to a private school.

Mercy High School is an incredibly special place that produces high caliber women of character. From day one until the day I graduated and beyond, the staff and faculty reminded me—no unabashedly told me—that women can do anything. When I graduated from Mercy, I took that foundation that women can do anything plus the extra special, intangible secret sauce with me to my predominately all-male, private military university.

Journal Exercise

1. Was there ever a time when you said *never*? Did it happen anyway? What was the outcome? Upon reflection, can you say it happened *for* you, or do you feel it happened *to* you and nothing good came from it?

2. Or journal about a time your parents sacrificed for you or put up with your shenanigans. Looking back at what they tolerated, does that give you a new appreciation for them and their love for you?

Life is about attitude and perspective. My first mentor in the military, Bruce, told me the only difference between having an adventure or an ordeal is attitude.

CHAPTER 8

THE STORY VERSUS THE FACTS

As I prepared to retire from the military, I asked myself: *What's next for me?* Working with my life coach, Leila, we began to explore different options. I shared with her that my undergraduate degree was in Civil Engineering. I then explained that I have never seen myself as a true engineer, so doing something in that field would be a backup plan to my backup plan.

I don't remember exactly what triggered the memory. Maybe she asked why I chose an engineering degree. After that call, I had a vivid memory of the pivotal moment when I decided to become an engineer. I also realized it was the story I made up and not the facts that drove me to become an engineer.

My sister graduated from college the summer before my junior year of high school. It was an important and huge celebration. Mom, Dad, and I traveled to the university to attend this massive graduation ceremony.

While watching the hundreds of graduates file into their seats, my slightly chauvinistic father said out loud, "Well, of course, that's the school of engineering filing in. There are no women in it."

I distinctly remember that Mom and I were mortified because he said it loud enough for others to hear, and I think I even elbowed him in his side. When it happened, I wondered if there were parents of a woman near us who heard his rude comment.

Looking back on that memory, I realize now, that was the exact moment I decided to become an engineer. Honestly, what my father said was factual. When I looked down to see the students filing in behind the School of Engineering sign, there were no women.

What did I hear? Or better yet: What was the story I made up? *Women can't be engineers.*

My father did not say to me, "Anela, you can't be an engineer because you are a woman."

But that sure is what I heard, or completely made up as a fabricated story, on that day. There is no doubt for me that subconsciously I decided right then—*I will show you, Dad! I will be an engineer!*

Don't get me wrong. I am proud of my Bachelor of Science in Civil Engineering degree. I have often joked that no one was more surprised than me the day they handed me my diploma. It was a long, hard-fought journey to earn that degree in four years. I even failed my first class ever while earning that degree. However, failing the class didn't really phase me because the *story* that women can't be engineers fueled my drive to finish in four years.

When I failed the class, I resigned myself to the fact that I must attend summer school in order keep my three-year Army Reserve Officers' Training Corps scholarship and graduate on time. (It turned out to be the best thing to happen to me. Check out the next chapter to learn how.)

Coming to that realization as an adult was eye-opening and surprising. I chose my course of study from a story I made up while attending a college graduation, six years before I graduated from college. Where else in my life had I made decisions from a story and not the facts? And how did those stories play a role in me becoming all I can be?

Journal Exercise

1. Think about the sheer power of the story you made up about something that happened in your life. Can you pull out the facts from the story you have told yourself? Write down the facts.

2. How has that story shaped your actions and your thoughts? Has the story helped you or held you back?

3. After separating the facts from the story, notice if you feel differently about that incident. Is there more space around what happened when you look at it from this perspective?

4. Can you find compassion for the other person involved? More importantly, can you find compassion for yourself and everything that was created by living from the story?

5. How did the story shape your becoming all you can be?

CHAPTER 9

Everything Happens For You

When I was a sophomore at Norwich University (a private military college), I took a required core engineering course called Dynamics. I took and passed the prerequisite course, Statics, and dreaded signing up for Dynamics. The Dynamics instructor, Professor Wallace, or "Wally" as he was affectionally called, was infamous campus wide for his teaching style. He was tough, and when he died after teaching at Norwich for more than fifty years, hundreds of students wrote about his antics and shared how much he was revered and loved.

From the first day of Dynamics, I knew I was in trouble. Every class, I showed up, took a quiz I didn't pass, took copious notes, and fell further behind. He assigned extra credit problems, and even that did not help me. It was all a foreign language. None of it made any sense. Additionally, I didn't have a study partner or study group as I did not appreciate how important or helpful that was.

By the end of the course, I needed a miracle to ace the final to pass the class with a D. For the first time in my academic career, I failed. While I knew it was coming, I had to wait until after summer break started to find out officially. I was devastated and disappointed in myself. The most embarrassing part was the fact that I had to go to summer school.

Much to my surprise, I could not have been more wrong. Summer school was the *best* thing that happened to me in college. It was amazing, and most importantly, it was fun. During the summer, I didn't have to wear uniforms. There were no room inspections. I didn't have to share my room with a roommate. The upper parade ground—which was sacred ground, grass you did not step foot on during the academic year—became a place to picnic, sunbathe, and play frisbee. Additionally, there was a world-renowned Russian School that took place every summer at Norwich, so there were hundreds of civilians all speaking Russian, wandering the campus. It was as if I were attending a *normal* college.

As great as all that was, the absolute best part of summer school was meeting a fellow student named Doug. I had seen him in the engineering building, so I knew he was one year ahead of me and was studying engineering. What I didn't know was he was also a civil engineering student and, due to a switch in majors, was going to end up graduating with my class.

He also purposefully did not take Prof. Wallace's Dynamics course because he knew from other students that it was better to take the course during summer school. So, my theory that everyone at summer school had failed was false. Unlike me, Doug was there by choice, and a smart choice it was. The summer school instruction was wonderful, and I understood each of the formulas, why they were important, and I even became interested in solving dynamics problems.

Most importantly, I began to study with Doug every single night. We became fast friends, and I began to understand engineering in a whole new way. I even enjoyed working on the problems together. He would understand one part of the problem, and I would understand the other part. Together, we would discover the whole answer.

We were each supportive, mostly patient, and we laughed at each other as we figured out each assignment. It was a perfect college study partner match, only made possible by my failing Dynamics during the regular school year.

I could not foresee that failing my first class would provide me with one of my greatest gifts. To this day, I remain friends with Doug and his wonderful family. The day we graduated, I gave much credit to him, and I still say that I would not be a civil engineer without Doug. We spent the next two years attached at the hip, studying almost every single night together. Failing the class brought me one of my best college experiences and one of my best friends in the world.

While I have many more stories that demonstrate that everything happens *for* me, this one is the first and my favorite.

Journal Exercise

1. Take a moment to think about something you *failed*. Can you see the gift in it now? Sit quietly and ask yourself what the gift was. Often, there is more than one gift.
2. Does everything happen *for* you or *to* you?

The next time you find yourself believing you have *failed*, take a deep breath and remember: *This, too, is happening for me. All is well. Everything is working out for me.*

The gift is there, I promise you, even in the toughest of situations. Trust that, and it will reveal itself to you. Everything happens *for* you.

CHAPTER 10

A MOMENT IN TIME

When I was a junior in college, I was hand-selected to represent my university at an Army convention that is now known as the largest military exposition and professional development forum in North America. At that time, it was held in the huge ballrooms of the Sheraton Hotel in downtown Washington, DC. Today, it fills the entire DC convention center. It is an enormous event and displays everything from the smallest piece of military gear, such as an ear plug, to the largest tank. For a junior in college, it was overwhelming, impressive, and lots of fun.

How did I get to attend? Each year, three private military colleges, Virginia Military Institute, the Citadel, and Norwich University shared a recruiting booth at this massive convention. In those days, only Norwich allowed women in their Corps of Cadets, and I was honored to be asked to represent my university.

We wore our class uniforms when working at the booth, and in the evenings, we attended formal dinners in our dress uniforms. While I had the option to wear pants in both uniforms, I chose to wear my skirt due to the warm weather. For me, the decision to wear a skirt was about comfort.

I can honestly say that I never gave that uniform decision too much thought—until an unexpected encounter. It was lunchtime, and my fellow classmates and I decided to leave the hotel for lunch. My everyday class uniform consisted of a short sleeve white shirt, a gray polyester skirt that fell to one inch above my knees, nude-colored nylons, and shiny black patent leather two-inch heels. I had noticeably short hair, small gold ball earrings, no make-up, and no nail polish. In my estimation, my attire wasn't all that feminine, but I certainly stood out since I wasn't wearing pants.

As we left the convention center, we passed through two sets of double doors. While I was in the vestibule, between the two sets of doors, I noticed a woman walking towards me wearing a dark business suit. She made direct eye contact with me and smiled a broad smile. I was a bit embarrassed as it seemed like she knew me. I smiled at her and quickly looked away, having absolutely no idea who she was. Before the second set of doors closed behind me, she turned around and walked out the same door I did. She politely stopped me by asking me if I had a minute.

While I thought it was strange, she was still smiling broadly. I said, "Yes, Ma'am."

I don't remember every single word she said to me, but I do vividly remember the message. That day, her actions gave more weight to what she said than her actual words. Her advice was so important to her that she turned around, followed me out of the building, got my attention, and asked me to stop. One tiny moment in time with a complete stranger.

How many people bother to go to those lengths for someone they do not know? I was aware enough to know that whatever she had to say was important and would probably have an impact on me. We didn't introduce ourselves; she simply commented on how feminine I looked in uniform.

While I thought that was strange, too, I smiled and had the presence of mind and military manners to say, "Thank you, Ma'am."

She went on to say in so many words: look around, femininity is not a trait you see often in the military. Then she highly encouraged me to maintain that quality when I entered active duty. She said I would lead young women, teenagers who would take their cues from me. She warned that they would always be watching me and recommended I be the role model of a strong feminine soldier for them to look up to, for them to emulate. By doing so, I would give them permission to be both strong and feminine.

That was it; that was all she wanted me to know. She thanked me for my time and walked back into the building while I scurried away to join my classmates at the restaurant. I can't honestly say I deeply appreciated all that she was trying to convey to me that day. I did not grasp the depth of it, the complexity of it, or the sheer importance of it. Still, her efforts and words opened my mind and caused me to be more observant and more aware of my actions.

About eighteen months later, it was time to graduate, and my academic advisor, Professor Burton, sat me down for our last counseling session before I walked across the stage to receive my diploma. We had a wonderful working relationship, and I viewed him as one of my favorite mentors.

We met when I was a freshman, and his mentorship led me from being an undecided engineer to a Civil Engineer major. He was a civil engineer and exceedingly kind. He took me under his wing, protected me, guided me, and genuinely cared about me and my academic success. I knew I could go to him for sage advice no matter the topic.

Among the many accolades he showered on me that day, he took a few minutes to talk about my one quality that most impressed him. He said that Norwich, like the military, was a harsh place, filled with relentless rigor, exacting discipline, and strict regulations. The school was unforgiving to nonconformity and male-dominated. He went on to say that in all the years that he had taught at Norwich, he had never met a woman who was able to balance her femininity with her strength and leadership in the way I had all four years I was in the Corps of Cadets.

He pointed out that throughout all my challenges and successes in and out of the classroom and the Corps of Cadets, it appeared that I had effortlessly maintained my feminine stature. He assured me that it was one of my greatest strengths, and he strongly encouraged me to maintain this special character trait once on active duty.

After the encounter at the convention, I did take time to look around and pay more attention to the women I met both in the military and the female cadets who attended Norwich before me. Many of them, not all, looked masculine in their appearance. Some had extremely short haircuts like the men and were bodybuilder-like in physical structure. These were tough women I would not want to run into in a dark alley at night and fierce enough to be on the front lines of combat. If I were picking a team to go into combat with, I would fight to have them in my unit.

I also paid more attention to how women interacted with me and how I interacted with them. I had never really thought of myself as a role model, and I took that more seriously after the anonymous woman stopped me and told me other women would look up to me.

In the military at that time, women generally treated other women harder and harsher because they didn't ever want to be accused of going too easy on a person because of gender. It is a tightrope we sometimes walk, and I started to care less about what others thought of my actions and more about being a good mentor, coach, and teacher.

After the second comment from my advisor, I realized there was something to this innate quality and I began to own it: not in an *in-your-face* kind of way, but in more of a *I can see that and its importance in me*. While I never chose my uniform skirt to flaunt my femininity, I was much more aware that when I wore it, I was presenting a way a young woman can show up and act while in uniform.

Throughout my career, I never really gave my gender much thought. Yes, I was different, and yes, my difference brought with it certain considerations. But for me, it was more important to walk into a room as a fellow soldier. I didn't lead with my femininity; it was a part of what I brought to the table. But it wasn't, in my mind, the quality that was most important.

I often remarked throughout my career that I would be halfway or sometimes all the way through a meeting before I would look around and realize I was the only woman at the table or the only woman in the room. While I am certainly proud to be a woman who served in the military, my gender was not what I wanted to be known for. It is a particularly important part of a much bigger whole.

There are many, many parts to a soldier. One size does not fit all, and it is our diversity, our disparate backgrounds, our multi-colored, multifaceted tapestry that is a huge part of what makes us the greatest military on the planet.

Journal Exercise

1. Have you ever shared a moment in time with a stranger to pay them a compliment or pass on sage advice? Has a stranger ever stopped you? If so, what was that experience like and how did you receive the information?
2. Do you consider yourself a role model? Whom have you already influenced?
3. What is a trait or characteristic that you may have downplayed or not realized? Is it important? Does it play a role in becoming all you can be?

CHAPTER 11

LYING IS A SIN

Growing up, Mom always told me lying is a sin. I associated a lot of guilt and heaviness with that statement, and yet, it did not stop me from lying to her. I never wanted to disappoint her, and sometimes found myself lying to her to avoid hurting her feelings, I thought. However, I was often caught in the lie. Something else she taught me: the truth always comes out, and honesty is the best policy.

When I was a senior in college, I was lucky enough to have my own room. I was authorized to have a small refrigerator, a lounging chair, and a TV. My parents had a small refrigerator that they let me take to school, and I had inherited a white reclining chair from an upperclassman, so all I needed was a TV. When I asked my parents about bringing a TV, Mom said no, absolutely not. She was adamant that it would be a distraction, and I needed to concentrate on my studies.

As I often did while growing up, I consulted my older sister who had more experience having been there and done that with my parents. She reminded me that I was a twenty-one-year-old adult, and if I wanted a TV, I had the money to purchase it. I remember getting off the call thinking she was right. A few days later, I bought a small twenty-inch television. I think it might have even been a black-and-white TV. I decided it was small enough to hide away when my parents came up for parents' weekend.

That was a great plan in theory except they arrived early that weekend, and I hadn't taken the time to hide it before I went to class. My sister was with them, and they all went to my room before I got back from class. It was a small dorm room, so there was no way Mom could miss the TV.

When I got back to my room, I could feel the tension in the air. She was so angry with me for lying to her. She kept saying she didn't care that I had the TV because I was an adult, but the fact that I didn't tell her I had one—that was a lie of omission. I felt terrible because I saw the anguish in her face and deeply felt her disappointment. To make matters worse, my sister spoke up on my behalf and, ultimately, was blamed for being a bad influence on me.

It tainted our last parents' weekend that included my parents presenting me my engraved cadet saber, which was an important and long-awaited rite of passage for every cadet officer. Only the officers in the Corps of Cadets are authorized to carry and use sabers in parades. It was something I had anticipated for three years, and the *TV lie* placed a heaviness on the excitement of receiving my saber.

A few weeks later, I received an exceedingly long, handwritten letter on yellow legal paper from my mom. I believe it is the longest letter I have ever received from her. In it, she spelled out in painstaking detail exactly how disappointed she was in me. While I don't remember all the details of the letter, what I do remember is that she had already bought me a TV for my dorm room, and she intended to give it to me along with the cadet saber. I had ruined her major surprise. A double whammy. It took her a long time to move past my lying to her. It took me a long time to get over disappointing her so deeply.

My lie of omission led to my mother's disappointment in me and a valuable lesson that honesty is the best policy. While I learned many lessons growing up, her words stung for a long time. Looking back, I realize this fear of disappointing others is one of the reasons I am still tempted to lie but choose not to.

It is ironic that I chose a profession where a person's word is their bond, and at work, I lived by values, such as honor and integrity. Integrity is key to living more consciously.

If you are lying to others or *out of integrity* with others, you are also lying to yourself and are out of integrity with yourself. How can you progress in any relationship, especially your relationship with yourself, if you aren't being honest with yourself? When you are out of integrity with yourself, it is difficult to align with your authentic self, the person you are at your core.

I have found that when I am honest—even when I fear it might hurt someone's feelings—most people appreciate knowing how I really feel. Even if they do not agree, they honor and respect my transparency, which demonstrates my willingness to be vulnerable.

Journal Exercise

1. Write about a time you lied to a friend or a family member.
2. What happened when you lied? How could you have avoided that outcome if you had been honest?

Consider making a commitment to speak your truth even if you fear that it will hurt the other person. There is a tremendous amount of respect that comes with speaking your truth.

CHAPTER 12

YOU ARE NEVER ALONE

I didn't buy my first car until after I graduated from college and was about to graduate from the US Army Engineer Officer Basic Course—a course that all new engineer officers must attend before their first assignment. The purchase was out of necessity. I was a second lieutenant on my way to my first assignment at Fort Carson, Colorado, and I had no wheels.

How I picked the car I decided to buy is totally my mother's fault, but that is another story for another time. Ironically, I ended up picking up my new car on Mom's birthday, and it was fun to have my parents with me that day.

It was a cold, wet day in March about a month shy of my twenty-third birthday. The day we went to the dealer to pick it up, Dad and I opened the trunk with the salesperson. He showed us the spare tire and where to find the jack. I also remember trying to pull the jack out to look at it, and when I wasn't able to, I distinctly remember thinking to myself: *I will figure that out if I ever need it.* Followed quickly with: *I pray I will never need it.*

It was a sporty car, low to the ground, two doors, and fast with a five-speed manual transmission. Why a manual five speed? Because Dad always told me, "You can't own a sports car with an automatic transmission."

I bought a Firestorm Red Dodge Stealth ES, and I love it. It is affectionately called *My Lieutenant Mobile*, and I am still driving it today.

Two days later, I drove my new car from St. Louis, Missouri, to Colorado Springs, Colorado. Talk about a fun drive—I-70 flat as a pancake and a 65 miles per hour speed limit in my new, bright red sports car!

A month later, I had moved into a one-bedroom apartment and started my first assignment as a brand-new platoon leader in charge of twenty-eight soldiers. It was my twenty-third birthday weekend, and I was feeling a little down, having to celebrate it all by myself for the first time.

I decided to make the most of the weekend by exploring a local attraction—the beautiful Royal Gorge Bridge and Park. It was only an hour away and seemed like a fantastic way to celebrate my special day. The trip to the gorge was uneventful and a pretty drive.

On my way to the bridge, I saw a sign for Cripple Creek and thought I might head there after checking out the home of America's highest suspension bridge. The bridge and gorge were breathtakingly gorgeous, and I felt good about making the trip; it lifted my spirits. As I headed back towards Colorado Springs, I decided to follow the sign to Cripple Creek. Why not? I was out, and I had heard others talk about the old gold mining camp turned casino town.

Let's keep the adventure going—

As I turned onto the two-lane road towards Cripple Creek, I noticed the speed limit slowly decrease, first down to 40, then 35 and finally down to 25 miles per hour. I thought that was odd and wondered why. Being a rules girl, I complied and soon understood why. The road to the town was in fact a dirt road. Not growing up near mountains, I didn't understand why it turned into a dirt road, but have since realized that many roads that climb up in elevation are often unpaved.

As I continued to drive 25 miles per hour, listening to the tiny rocks TINK as they bounced off the bottom of my brand-new sports car, I had an entire conversation with myself about taking my pristine, new car on this dirt road. I now realized why so many of my peers at Fort Carson owned trucks and jeeps. They were perfect for this kind of driving. I decided that I only had this one car, so if I was going to explore Colorado, I was going to do it in this car—so no need to baby it.

A short time later, I was driving along a picturesque stream. I remember saying a prayer to God, thanking Him for this beauty and saying this is exactly what I needed on my birthday. Shortly after that, I started to climb and climb and climb. I was grateful I was driving on the side closest to the mountain and not on the ledge side. At one point, I passed a truck that was stopped on the ledge side, but there was no driver.

I thought that was odd and wondered why it was there, since I also noticed it was a US Army Corps of Engineers truck with government license plates. Being a newly minted US Army Corps of Engineers officer, I took it as a good omen. Not long after passing that truck, I encountered a vehicle coming down the mountain towards me. Although there was plenty of room for both of us, I moved over towards the mountain slightly, out of courtesy.

POP! I hit a rock with the passenger side front tire. Having no idea how serious it was, I immediately pulled over. The car that passed me didn't know I had hit anything and kept driving.

I got out of the car and saw that the tire was completely flat. I would later find out I busted the sidewall when I hit the rock and needed a new tire. While I didn't completely panic (I knew on some level that panicking was wasted energy and wouldn't get me off the side of this mountain), I had a few thoughts floating through my mind. *God, didn't I just thank you for this beautiful drive? I have never ever changed a tire before! I am on the side of a mountain, in the middle of nowhere, all alone* (this was long before cell phones and GPS).

Then, being a good Army officer, I took action. I thought: *I have a manual. I am sure it will show me how to change a tire. I am a smart engineer; I can figure this out!*

Before I pulled out the manual, I decided the first thing I would do is figure out how to remove that jack in the trunk. Yep, I still had no idea how to get the jack out of the car. So, I spent my first fifteen to twenty minutes trying to figure that out. Eventually, it occurred to me that it was expanded to fit snugly in its compartment. As soon as I turned the knob to collapse the jack, it literally fell right out of the compartment.

I was so proud of myself and eager to use it. I pulled out the manual that said the first step was to loosen the lug nuts. For some reason, this engineer (or not-engineer in that moment) thought that didn't make sense, so I decided to jack the car up first. I know you are laughing as you are seeing a picture of the tire spinning freely as I tried to loosen the lug nuts.

Did I mention that my special sporty tires had a lug nut lock to boot? Yes, I quickly realized why you loosen the lug nuts before lifting the car off the ground. The stubborn Taurus in me decided I could get the tire off without lowering the car.

In that exact moment, God sent his angels to me. A wonderful and gracious elderly couple pulled up behind me and offered to help me. The driver saw that I only had the tiny L-shaped tire iron that came with the car. He tried to use it before he went to his truck to get his large four-way tire iron.

As he walked back from his truck, he remarked that it would be easier if we lowered the car. I laughed a little and explained that this was my first tire-changing experience. He nodded and smiled. He lowered the car and stood on his tire iron to get the lug nuts loose. He remarked how difficult an impact wrench makes changing a tire. I thanked him profusely and said I would never have been able to change the tire without his help.

The lug nut that required the special lock was the hardest to remove, but once the job was complete, he put on my 50-mph rated tiny, donut spare tire and placed the heavy flat tire in my trunk. He and his wife insisted that they follow me until we hit a paved road again. We didn't reach a paved road until we arrived in Cripple Creek.

I was so emotionally and physically exhausted that I did not stop. To this day, I have never explored that old gold-mining camp turned into a casino town. Really, I am not much of a gambler anyway, unless we are talking about driving a month-old sports car on a dirt road in the middle of the Colorado mountains. That gamble cost me $225. Yes, one sports car tire = $225.

Most importantly, I look back on that whole experience fondly as a powerful reminder that I am never alone. That amazing couple arrived at the exact moment when I needed the most help and stayed with me until I was out of danger.

You truly are never alone!

Journal Exercise

1. I invite you to think of a time when you were *stranded* or thought you could use some help. Did someone or something come along to help?

   Journaling about that time can be your personal evidence that you are never alone. I have since learned that there is a company of unseen angels that are always around you, and they can only help you if you ask them for help. If you do find yourself in an uncomfortable situation or stranded, ask for their help. They are standing by, waiting to be asked, and are eager to help you.

CHAPTER 13

LITTLE THINGS MATTER

When I was a young lieutenant, I deployed to Somalia. It was my first deployment, and I learned many professional and life lessons.

The day we deployed, my parents were there to see me off.

Mom tells the story that while she and Dad were standing on the tarmac, watching me board the plane, Dad said to her, "Did you ever imagine you would be here again?"

He was referring to the times she watched him deploy to Korea once and Vietnam twice. She looked at him with tears in her eyes and said, "No, I never imagined I would ever say goodbye to another deploying soldier, let alone my own daughter."

When she told me that story, it was the first time I stopped to imagine how hard it must be for a parent to support their child's desire to serve their country, knowing that their child may not come home. That is a tall order of any human, especially a parent.

My parents stood on the tarmac with a huge FAREWELL, LT ARCARI sign, and they stayed there late into the night until the plane finally took off. I watched the sun set in Colorado before we took off, and I watched the sun rise in Georgia when we landed to pick up more soldiers on the way to Somalia.

I watched the sun set in Ireland when we stopped to refuel. We were able to get off the plane and stretch our legs. We took off, and I watched the sun rise in Cairo where we stopped to refuel but were not allowed to get off the plane.

When we landed in Mogadishu around noon that day, it was bright and sunny, but the devastation I saw out the window was so shocking it literally took my breath away. I remember saying to myself: *How could humans do this to humans?* There were no doors or windows in any buildings and many roofs were destroyed, yet people were living in the ruins.

There were power poles but no power lines. I learned later that all the power lines were stripped for the copper. It was a war-torn country and not like anything I had ever seen before. I was so naive that I was nervous, but I don't remember feeling terrified or scared. Seventeen years later, when I landed in Kabul, Afghanistan, I knew enough to be so terrified I was shaking from head to toe.

After landing, we gathered our gear—affectionally called *battle rattle*, which consisted of a flack vest (heavy bulletproof vest) with ammo pouches, canteens, a first aid kit that included a tourniquet, a Kevlar helmet, and an M16 assault rifle with issued bayonet. It was hard flying on a commercial plane with all the gear stuffed into every available space in the overhead bins and under the seat in front of me. Fitting the thirty-nine-inch long M16 was by far the toughest item to store for the over thirty-six hour flight.

The tiny details that stayed with me are interesting. We didn't have any carry-on luggage, but every soldier on the plane had all that military gear with them, crammed into every available space.

We stayed at the airport until all our bags were unloaded from the plane. I was there long enough to watch the plane—my only way to escape the country—take off into the sunset. We had departed Colorado two nights before, and as I watched the plane take off, I had no idea how long we were going to be in this utterly destroyed city. I was still viewing the entire experience as an adventure.

Little did I know what was in store.

We claimed our two duffle bags and large ruck sack (backpack) and loaded them onto trucks. We then got in other trucks, and the entire convoy of gear and soldiers headed to our basecamp.

We traveled a long, straight road with the airport at one end and our basecamp at the other. The roads were dirt with many potholes, so the ride was bumpy, even though it was a main street in downtown Mogadishu, and it was very populated. We appeared ready for war, and the people of the city were going about their day-to-day business, shopping at the market, carrying water—surviving in the middle of the devastation all around them.

It was surreal. What planet had I landed on? It was so far from anything I'd witnessed in the United States. I tried to imagine one of the Somalians I saw as we drove by standing in a place like Times Square in New York City. I guessed it would blow their mind. How could these two places exist on the same planet?

When we arrived about twenty minutes later at our basecamp, the unit we were replacing *warmly* greeted us, because they were excited that their replacements had arrived, and they would be going home any day now. What a mix of emotions all in one place: their excitement, almost giddiness and our apprehension and fear of the unknowns.

I knew I would feel the same way when our replacements showed up, but I had no idea when that would be. When we deployed, they told us it could be six months or longer. This unit had been there about five months. Due to the exponential increase in hostilities, we only stayed four months. Those four months remain the closest I ever came to combat and the only time in my twenty-eight-year career when I did not think I was coming home alive.

While I never fired my weapon except on the range, most of my thirty-eight assigned soldiers found themselves in precarious situations that required them to defend their position and protect themselves. Through the grace of God, I was the only platoon leader who deployed with thirty-eight soldiers and returned home with thirty-eight soldiers. Also, through the grace of God, while some soldiers were sent home due to serious injuries, they all lived.

My first night, I was bunked with the only female officer from the unit we were replacing. Unlike me, she had already done her platoon leader time and was the company executive officer—the officer considered second in charge. If anything were to happen to the commander, the executive officer takes charge of the unit.

She was excited to meet me and happy to show me around. What I remember most about her was the way she threw on the flack vest like it was as light as a feather and her second skin. When I asked her about it, she said it would be no time at all before I did the same thing. I didn't believe her, but she was right. Within weeks, it was as natural and easy as putting on a wind breaker. My body was amazing and resilient as it adjusted to the additional weight, all while experiencing a mere 90–120°F degrees during the day.

Although there are many other incredible and different first impressions, one of my first additional duties I was assigned was that of postal officer and morale, welfare, and recreation (MWR) officer. Being the postal officer was easy. I had two soldiers who helped me pick up the mail daily from the quartermaster unit and, later each day, helped me distribute the mail. I had heard how important mail is to a soldier, but until I witnessed the joy of seeing a soldier receive mail, any mail (it does not matter who it is from), the sheer importance cannot be adequately described or explained.

As vital as a letter might be, you cannot fathom the incredible impact a care package brings. Not only did I see the reactions of each soldier as they heard their name called and stepped forward to grab the letter or the package, I experienced my own reaction at receiving a card from Mom and Dad or a care package from my sister. To this day, my sister's chocolate chip cookies or my Mom's from-scratch brownies have never, will never taste as good as they did when sent to me all over the world during my deployments.

The MWR duties weren't necessarily hard; I just didn't know where to start to bring some fun into the monotony of downtime between missions. The unit we replaced had built a makeshift basketball court that was popular for pick-up games. It occurred to me that it might be fun to host a basketball tournament between our engineer unit and the quartermaster unit located next to us.

I remember worrying that there might not be enough interest to fill brackets for a tournament. Never did I imagine that one little basketball tournament would have such an impact. I also remember sitting down at one of the three computers we had in the entire unit to create a simple slide to use as posters to announce the upcoming competition. The slide was so basic—black and white, nothing special, nothing fancy—but it was key to getting the message out.

The outpouring of responses was overwhelming. This tournament idea—that I thought was small and inconsequential—took on a life of its own. More and more teams came forward, and the tournament I initially planned for one morning turned into a three-day event. After the basketball tournament, we moved onto a volleyball tournament that garnered the same level of enthusiasm and participation.

That quartermaster unit we competed against was responsible for feeding us three meals a day and brought our mail from the airport to the basecamp each day, among many other important tasks. Their mission was as critical as ours, and we built comradery and lifelong friendships through sports during that deployment.

I share all of this to provide a small glimpse of what it is like to deploy while serving in the military. It is unlike anything else I experienced, and as difficult as it can be, it is also an incredibly special and sacred time, one that can't be replicated or understood unless personally experienced.

I share this story to also remind you that the little things do count. I still handwrite letters and send postcards because of the joy I witnessed each time we held mail call in the middle of a combat zone in Mogadishu. Connecting with people across town and across great distances—it matters. Not only does it matter, but it also makes a difference beyond anything you can imagine.

Likewise, incorporating fun into everything you do brings joy, and joy brings abundance and generosity. I have recently taken up the practice of turning on some music and dancing at work in the middle of the most stressful part of my day. Even if only for thirty seconds to a minute. Disrupting the business with the sheer enjoyment of dance puts everything into perspective and uncannily calms everything down. If dancing is not for you, then incorporate something that brings you joy. You will be amazed how even something short or small can shift the entire energy and environment for the rest of the day.

Journal Exercise

1. What are some of the small or big things you do that make a difference?
2. In what ways do you incorporate joy and fun into your day?

They say one of the quickest ways to lift your spirits is to do an act of kindness for someone else. Maybe try that the next time you are in need of a quick pick-me-up.

CHAPTER 14

TAKE THE FIRST STEP

Flashback: I am standing in a wide-open space, entirely unprotected from the enemy. I am completely frozen, in time and space—unable to take one step.

Where am I and how did I get here? I am in Somalia, in a combat zone where the lives of my soldiers are absolutely on the line, or so I believe in that moment. As their platoon leader, their lives depend on my decisions and my orders. They look to me and the platoon sergeant to care for them and their families.

It is an enormous responsibility and an incredible honor. Did I mention I am only twenty-four years old in charge of thirty-eight soldiers, half a million dollars' worth of equipment, and I am in a combat zone? While officially it is a United Nations (UN) humanitarian mission, in three months, we have gone from an average of three to five attacks against the UN forces to an average of over thirty each week.

As mentioned in the previous chapter, my deployment in Somalia was the closest I ever came to combat in my twenty-eight years and the only time I was not sure I would come home alive. I genuinely feared for my life. So much so, I sat quietly one day and reviewed my life, asking myself if I had any regrets. At that time in my young life, I only had one. I vowed if I made it out alive, I would reach out to that person and make amends, which I did.

On this day, a messenger came to my living area that also served as my office to tell me that the company commander needed to see all the platoon leaders immediately. The soldier explained that there was a credible report that our base camp would soon be attacked by over 200 angry Somalians.

The messenger left, I threw on my flak vest that had become my second skin, slung my weapon over my back, grabbed my notebook, and headed out the door. My door was maybe sixty feet (about twenty-five steps) from the door of our command post or headquarters. The command post was an abandoned, run down, and looted home that happened to be white, so it was affectionately and sarcastically called "The White House"—not very original as that is what it literally was, a white house.

The very short walk was across a completely open, flat dirt area and was right in front of the main gate into our basecamp. The gate where presumably over 200 angry Somalians would soon be trying to breach our secured *safe haven*. As I walked towards The White

House, I looked at the main gate, and I imagined 200 angry men and boys climbing up and around the gate.

In my mind, I saw the gate completely overrun by an angry mob within minutes, and I thought: *How will we defend against that?* With that image in my head, I froze. I was about twelve steps into my walk, or about halfway between the two doors, and I stopped. I *froze* in place, unable to move in any direction.

I began to shake from my head to my toes. I had never been this scared in my life, and my nervous system was desperately trying to process the inconceivable image that filled my brain. My body's initial response was not fight-or-flight, it was to freeze in place and shake uncontrollably.

I stood there for what seemed like minutes but was probably only a few seconds and thought: *How will I put one foot in front of the other? I am completely immobile, and my feet will not budge.*

I am in the open, I thought, knowing that anyone in the buildings that looked down into our basecamp could take me out in an instant. One shot and I would be hit and maybe even dead. Not even that thought jarred me. I was frozen and could not will myself to move. As my body continued to shake, I began to feel nauseous, as I once again imagined hordes of people pouring over and through the gate. Internally, I reprimanded myself, screaming to just take the first step, but I could not do it.

Then, a vision came into my mind. Behind me, in the building I just walked out of, were several of my soldiers. Without turning around, I knew they were looking out the door and window at me, watching me, waiting with bated breath to see what my next action, or literally what my next step was going to be. That image hit the back of my head like a two-by-four, and I knew I had to find it in me to take a step as calmly as I could possibly manage.

Knowing they were staring at my back, I found the courage to take the first step and then another. It took every ounce of courage not to run to the door of The White House. That would have been a flight response—run, run as fast as you can to safety, cover, and protection.

Luckily, from a previous experience, I knew that if I did that, I would not only confirm their fears, but panic would spread like a wildfire throughout the entire platoon. If I maintained a calm, cool, collected, level head, then they would do the same. Leaders set the tone, always. While I had no idea how we would manage an attack of that size, I did know all I had to do was put one foot in front of the other until I was inside The White House where I would receive the plan and my orders.

In that instance, I found the bravery to take one step forward when every single cell in my body was screaming at me to do the opposite. Life, any journey, or story begins with the first step and only unfolds in the present moment. The courage that I gathered in that moment stayed with me forever and still plays a vital role in my becoming all I can be.

I've learned that if I try to figure out all the steps before I take the first step, I am often overwhelmed. I've found that when I take the first step with full confidence and faith, the second step can be revealed. And when I take the second step with full confidence and faith, the third step can be revealed. Before I know it, I've reached my goal.

The harder the first step is to take, the more important it is for you to take it. While I appreciate that your first step will most likely not be in a combat situation, it doesn't make it any less critical.

Journal Exercise

1. Is there a time when you froze and didn't know what to do next?
2. What did you do to muster the courage to take the next step?
3. How important is that first step? Where did that one step take you?

CHAPTER 15

EQUIFINALITY

Equifinality is one of my favorite words. I could bore you with the whole scientific definition, but in simple terms, it is the principle that in open systems a given end state can be reached by many potential means. I first heard this word when I was earning my master's degree in a class about change management. It was explained in this way: if you have a point A and point B is your end state, there are an infinite number of ways to move from point A to point B. It was further described: Imagine point A is birth and point B is death—there are an infinite number of ways to choose to live your life.

When I first heard the word, I thought about my sister and her path to live a life she really loved and my path to do the same. What hit me was the fact that my path does not match my sister's path or anyone else's path, and that is completely acceptable and even expected! Equally important, I also realized that if our paths are unique to each individual, then there is no reason to fall into the trap of comparison.

A few years before I attended graduate school, my sister started to attend inspirational events all over the country. It seemed like every time we talked, she would pass on some great nugget of wisdom she had learned from these events. She was so excited, and I could see they were making a difference in her life, and she really wanted me to attend an event with her.

While I appreciated the valuable information she shared, I am not sure why, but I did not feel attending was something that was right for me. After many requests, my parents and I attended an event held in a large arena with eight to ten thousand participants. It was my first event like this, so it was overwhelming with lots of loud music and people dancing all around the arena. While it was a fun atmosphere, it was chaotic and unnerving for this newbie to the world of personal transformation live events.

That day, several guests shared their stories of how they came to be living lives they really enjoyed. All the concepts I heard that day did speak to me as I believed in my heart that there was *more to life* than getting up, going to work, coming home, and repeating like *Groundhog Day.*

At that time, though, that style of learning didn't appeal to me. I felt most of it was a hard sell to buy this course or that book. I was turned off by most of the event. I do remember buying a book and audio program, bringing it home, and having it collect dust on my bookcase for years because I was too busy to make the time to do the course.

After that opportunity with my sister, I felt bad that I didn't follow her path. Honestly, for several years, I felt that I had let my sister down by not following her suggested way. I also wondered if I had screwed up and somehow lengthened my journey by not attending.

Then I learned one simple word—equifinality. And in that moment, I felt a freedom I hadn't previously experienced. Not only did it apply to my relationship with my sister, but there were several other areas in my life where I had thought there was only one path or had fallen into the trap of comparing my life to someone else's.

Maybe you have heard or read this before, but I am here to say it again in yet another way: *You are on your very own unique path, as unique as your fingerprint.* Because your journey is unique, no amount of comparison is ever going to help you. In my experience, the sooner I appreciate the beauty of my path, the easier the journey becomes because I am expending my precious energy on my unique, made-only-for-me path.

I did go home after that event and continue my personal growth in a much quieter, much more comfortable way—mostly reading books on my own. As an introvert, quiet reading seemed more my style and was certainly easier than dancing in front of eight thousand strangers.

Although, you should see me now. I am up on stage leading the dancing these days.

As I thought about my own search for personal growth, or at least my individuality, the idea that there are an infinite number of ways to reach my point B set me free. Part of the past dynamic with my sister and many other friends included me falling into the pit of spending time comparing my path to anyone else's.

Journal Exercise

1. Have you ever compared your path to someone else's?
2. Have you thought you were ahead or behind when you compared?
3. How did comparing help you? Did comparing hold you back?
4. How does the understanding of equifinality help or hinder the habit of comparing?

CHAPTER 16

THE POWER OF HELLO

Too often we underestimate the power of a touch,
a smile, a kind word, a listening ear, an honest
compliment, or the smallest act of caring, all of which
have the potential to turn a life around.
—Leo Buscaglia

This beautiful quote reminds me of a story that circulated in emails in early 2000 about the boy walking home from high school with all his books from his locker and a fellow student who offered to help carry the books.

The story goes on to say that they became best friends. When they graduated, the boy with all the books revealed that because his now best friend said hello and offered to help the day they met, he decided not to take his life that night. *Never underestimate the power of kindness or a simple hello.*

In July 2000, I, too, had the privilege of experiencing a chance encounter that, nineteen years later, would remind me of this email story about the power of saying hello.

That summer, thanks to the Army, I had just earned my master's degree in counseling and leadership development. As part of the agreement for having the Army pay for that degree, my next assignment was at the United States Military Academy at West Point to utilize my newly learned skills.

I supported Cadet Basic Training, affectionately known as "Beast Barracks." During these first six weeks, West Point indoctrinated the newest class into the military way of life, learning basic skills, such as marching, physical training, basic first aid, land navigation, and marksmanship.

For many of the students, it was the first time they had ever used a compass or held a rifle. For some of these eighteen-year-olds, it was a significant shock to their system, and some decided to leave. Since there were no less than one hundred applicants for every available slot at West Point, the selection process to pick the absolute best candidates was rigorous, time consuming, and thorough.

Therefore, when a new cadet decided that they no longer wished to be at West Point, the exit process was almost as rigorous and extremely thorough. The academy wanted to give the new cadet every chance before they made such a final and irrevocable decision. As part of the exit process, at least four different people at each level of the chain of command counseled the departing cadet for a total of six to eight interviews.

Since this was my first exposure to summer training, the academy required me to shadow a seasoned officer who had at least one year under his belt. As a newbie, the duty of being the first Army officer to counsel a cadet wishing to leave fell to me.

The only real guidance I remember receiving was, "See what you can do to change their mind. We really don't want to lose any cadets this early in the process."

The night before my first counseling interview, I could not sleep as I tried to think of something ingenious to say to put them at ease and something clever to convince them to stay. In the end, I decided to be me, speak from the heart, keep an open mind, and, more importantly, listen from the heart.

Until they sat down with me, the only people they had talked to were upper-class students assigned as their squad leader, platoon sergeant, platoon leader, and company commander—positions filled by two juniors and two seniors at the academy.

By the time they saw me, they had their reasons down pat. Yet, I was the first Active Duty Officer they spoke to—an officer in the rank of Captain with nine years of service and experience. To say that it was daunting for some of them to sit down with me is an understatement. I understood this reality so it was important to me to do my best to put them at ease so we could have an honest conversation about what was going on.

While I can't tell you how many departing cadets I talked with that summer, I can tell you about two young women I met during those counseling sessions. I remained in touch with both of them for many years.

The first one, Katie, had the opportunity to take a four-year Naval ROTC scholarship at Georgetown University or attend West Point. In the end, she decided to give the academy a chance and quickly realized within the first two weeks she really wanted to go to a *normal* school and enjoy her college years. She was determined to be a lawyer, and she knew that the Navy ROTC scholarship was still available, as was her acceptance at Georgetown.

I distinctly remember being extremely impressed by her poise, confidence, intellect, and solid plan going forward. I had no misgivings about her decision to leave. I offered to stay in touch with her, and she said she would take me up on that offer. For several years, we exchanged Christmas letters, and I was not surprised when she graduated from law school and went into the Navy.

The second young woman I met was Roxanne. She, on the other hand, did not come across as confidently and did not, in my opinion, have a solid plan. I felt assured she had what it took to make it at the academy, and she was adamant that even without a backup plan it was time for her to go home.

I was worried about Roxanne and her future. I also offered to stay in touch with her and can't honestly say I expected that we would. However, Roxanne and I did exchange Christmas cards and even an occasional letter or card during the year. She went back to Arkansas, while I continued to move around the world, so we skipped some years here and there. Toward the end of our communication, we went a good ten years without any contact.

While I don't remember all the details, it seemed from her letters that Roxanne struggled for a few years and at one point was in a serious car accident. I continued to worry about her and was extremely proud and happy when she became a pharmacist.

In 2019, I was getting ready to retire after twenty-eight years of service. I planned a huge celebration of service at the Smithsonian Castle in Washington, DC, and I wanted to invite all the people I could who had helped or had an impact on me and my career. As I mentally went through each assignment, both Katie and Roxanne came to mind when I recalled my time at West Point.

I hit Google and social media to find email addresses for both. While I didn't hear back from Katie, I did hear from Roxanne. She received the invitation but had missed the response date because she was on vacation in Scotland. When she contacted me, the ceremony was less than a week away, and she explained that she wanted to come and asked me if it was too late.

I was in awe. I still am to this day. Roxanne and I shared one in-person conversation for twenty minutes in 2000, and in 2019, she enthusiastically wanted to attend my retirement ceremony. How incredible!

In the days leading up to the ceremony, I decided not to write out a speech, but to talk from my heart. When I thought about what I wanted to say about Roxanne's presence at my ceremony nineteen years after we last saw each other, I remembered the email and the power of kindness, the power of simply saying hello.

The night before the ceremony, I wondered if I would even recognize her. Luckily, I would be wearing my uniform, so it would be easy for her to recognize me. I did recognize her as soon as I saw her. We walked towards each other and gave each other a big hug as if no time had passed between us. It was surreal. She shared with me what an incredible impression I made on her all those years ago and how grateful she was that our paths crossed that day. I shared how immensely proud of her I was. It was amazing.

Would you believe I forgot to mention her in my retirement speech? I panicked when I realized it as we transitioned from the ceremony to the reception. I remembered we were going to do a champagne toast halfway through the reception. I had told Dad he would kick off the toasts, so I found him and said I had a few toasts I wanted to make first. When it came time for the toasts, I asked Roxanne to come stand next to me, and

I told the amazing story of us by starting with, "Never, never underestimate the power of saying hello. . ."

You are a bright light that shines every day. Even when you do not feel like you are shining your light—you are. Know that you create impressions and make impacts even when you aren't purposefully doing so. *Hello* is powerful. Never underestimate the act, and if called to say hello, offer a compliment, help a stranger—consider listening to the calling and act.

Journal Exercise

1. Think of a time when a small act of kindness made an impression on you. If you are moved by that time, consider journaling about that moment, what transpired, what made it so meaningful, and what about it causes you to remember it.
2. If you feel called, reach out to that person, let them know, and thank them. Don't be surprised if within days of completing this exercise, you hear from that person or if someone who feels the same way about you suddenly reaches out to you to thank you.
3. If it is not possible to reach out, consider writing a letter to that person about your experience and expressing your gratitude.

CHAPTER 17

INTO THE NEWS

One week after September 11, 2001, America reacted to another threat—anthrax. Why do I remember that day and that event? That was the day that I made the decision—no, the choice—to stop watching the news.

On September 11, I was living one hour north of *Ground Zero* in New York City. I was safe, living on a military installation that shut its gates that day for security reasons due to the attacks. Yet that night, I distinctly remember walking around my second-floor apartment, making sure all my doors and windows were locked. I knew it was irrational, and yet it was the only thing I could think of doing to bring myself some sense of control and security.

Earlier that morning, I watched the events live and was in shock as the second plane hit the second tower. Then every night like most Americans, I was glued to my TV, watching the horror of that day play over and over again. I crawled into bed each night alone and afraid, wondering: *What is next?* or *How can we move forward from such a devastating event?*

Then on September 18, 2001, newscasters took to the airwaves with the answer to my *What's next?* question when they announced the first of several letters laced with anthrax were delivered that day. I distinctly remember sitting on my couch, staring at the TV, and feeling completely and totally terrified in my own home.

Who was behind these insidious attacks only days after passenger planes became weapons? It was as if someone decided to answer the question: How can it get any worse than this? Lace some envelopes with poison and put them in the mail. Who does that when a nation is already reeling from such devastation? I had no answers as fear wracked my brain. I felt helpless, and the situation seemed hopeless.

Sitting in that fear, I realized: *I* did that. Only me. I invited the newscasters into my home, my sanctuary, my safe space. And as quickly as I realized that I was responsible for their presence in my living room, I turned the TV off and vowed I would no longer watch the news.

I remember thinking: *No one gets to come into my personal space and scare the living crap out of me, NO ONE!* For me, it was a defining moment, a moment when I took back my power to create a space in which I truly felt safe. A moment to honor my sacred needs for comfort, security, and support. It was empowering and liberating and scary, all at the same time. I was an officer in the United States Army.

As a leader, I had to keep up to date in current affairs. It was my duty and expected.

However, early in my career, I did not watch the news on a regular basis. When the Marines hit the beaches off the coast of Mogadishu, Somalia, in December 1992, I was completely caught off guard when my unit received orders in February 1993 to deploy to Somalia in six weeks. I was one year out of college, just twenty-three years old, in charge of thirty-eight soldiers, preparing to take them into a hostile situation, and because I had not been following the events happening in Somalia, I was— or at least I felt at the time—completely uninformed and unprepared.

How could I possible lead America's sons and daughters into combat when I had not even paid attention to how we got to this point where the military was being called in to help deliver food to starving people? In that moment in 1993, I swore the opposite—I would watch the news every day because I would never be caught off guard like that again. If someone had told me that one day I would decide to stop watching the news, I would not have believed it and would have thought that seemed like a drastic solution. I believed it was my duty to watch the news. It was an intricate part of my success in my job.

And yet, I kept my vow that I made on 18 September 2001, and I did not watch the news on a daily basis—not the local news, not the national news, and not the 24/7 cycles of cable news stations. What I quickly discovered was that if something big happened in the news, someone would tell me about it.

I have never missed a large story, such as an attack on deployed soldiers, the tragedy of a mass shooting, the death of a president, the impending landfall of a hurricane, or the announcement of a royal wedding or birth. If called to, once someone tells me about a big story, I will turn on the TV or look up a headline to learn a bit more. Then, I drop it. I don't hold onto it. I don't play it over and over again. I don't put my attention on it.

Why not put my attention on it? What is the effect of watching or reading something repeatedly?

The answers to those questions started to form in October 2006, when I first came to understand the concept or what I call a *universal truth*: what you put your attention on, grows. That is when I first watched the movie *The Secret*, which lays out The Law of Attraction in a succinct and powerful way. While I thought my decision to stop watching the news in 2001 was self-centered and about self-preservation, it turned out I was choosing where to focus my attention and choosing what I wished to see grow in my life.

Then in January 2020, I attended an inspirational retreat. During that amazing and inspiring three-day event, one of the presentations talked about being careful how you choose to spend your time and energy and what you choose to put your attention on. The presenter brilliantly demonstrated this critical point using an incredible slide that showed a thumbnail picture of several different *Time* magazine covers. One by one, each cover populated the slide with headlines of global warming, gun control, racism, women's equality, the effects of stress, and tensions in the Middle East. I thought, as did the majority of the audience, they were recent 2019–2020 covers.

Imagine our shock when the presenter revealed all those covers were thirty years old. The presenter pointed out that these stories continue to be perpetuated because we direct our attention on them instead of taking action. Think about that. Our major headlines have not changed much in over thirty years.

That revelation stopped me in my tracks and validated my personal commitment not to be *into the news* all those years ago. While I thought my choice was about protecting myself and creating a sense of security, I realized it was instead a powerful decision to choose what I wish to see grow in my life, which was *not* the same sensationalized stories over and over again.

Please do not misread this; I am not saying stick your head in the sand and ignore what is going on. Absolutely not. If one of those issues that has not changed in thirty years speaks to you, then become an advocate for change, placing your energy and attention on viable solutions and concrete actions that will move the issue forward.

For example, Mother Theresa was once asked when she would join the anti-war protest, and she basically responded, *as soon as it becomes a peace rally*. In other words, be for something, get involved in sacred activism.

Choose carefully exactly where you place your precious energy and attention so that it grows in the direction of positive change and does not get stuck in the *do loop* of the thirty plus years news cycle.

Journal Exercise

1. Are there areas in your life where you put a lot of attention and energy that might not be areas you wish to see grow? What are they?
2. How can you shift your focus and energy to areas you do wish to see grow and expand?

CHAPTER 18

CHANGE YOUR ATTITUDE, CHANGE THE OUTCOME

When I was thirty-four years old, I received orders for my first year-long deployment. Up until that point, all my deployments were less than six months long and never occurred during Christmas.

While I knew there was a possibility I would deploy during the holidays, I hoped it wouldn't happen to me. When I realized it would be my first Christmas away from my parents and family in my life, I felt sad. I arrived in Kuwait in August, and anytime I thought about spending the holidays away from home, I felt upset and depressed.

I had missed Thanksgiving before while deployed to Haiti, so that wasn't a big deal. The efforts the military goes through to ensure all deployed service members have turkey on Thanksgiving Day is remarkable. I know the Army tracks the shipment of every single turkey from the time the order goes into the supply system until it arrives at every single remote location. The spread and elaborate decorations on Thanksgiving are something to behold. All the effort the dining facilities put forth definitely takes the sting out of being so far from home.

My mom sent the best care packages anytime I deployed. She is the consummate Army wife and Army mom. She once sent Dad lasagna all the way to Korea, and she sent me more than one birthday cake with ingredients to make my own frosting. Amazingly, some cakes made it, but some cakes did not. It was always the thought that counted.

Thanksgiving at Camp Doha, Kuwait, came and went without much ado. Then, I received two large boxes from Mom. These two boxes were filled with Christmas decorations. The boxes were big and awkward and one of my co-workers, Bob, helped me carry them to my trailer.

As we were walking across the compound, we heard liquid sloshing and Bob said, "There is alcohol in this box."

I immediately denied it, saying alcohol was not allowed and my parents would never send anything that would get me in trouble. Under General Order Number One, we were in a country that didn't allow alcohol, so we weren't allowed to have any for the duration of the deployment out of respect to our host nation.

My father was a retired veteran and would never break the rules—or so I thought. Bob insisted it was alcohol, and I insisted it was not. It is a good thing I didn't take a bet because I would have lost.

My parents sent me some shelf-stable eggnog in a can that didn't need to be refrigerated until opened. Dad thought eggnog should have a little shot of something and packed a small glass jar, like a spice jar, filled with a shot of brandy to add to my eggnog. He then hid the jar inside a wood putty can. When I looked at it, I thought: *How did Dad know I am required to fill all the holes in the walls when I move out of my trailer?*

I laughed out loud when I realized what was really inside the can. Here I thought my Dad was a rules guy, and he had sent me contraband. I immediately worried I would get in trouble, but I felt that if he went through all that trouble, I should at least save it for Christmas night and enjoy some spiked eggnog—thanks to his rebel side.

On a side note, I kept it well hidden until Christmas night. Before going to bed, I poured myself some eggnog and a small amount of brandy. Not being much of a drinker, it tore up my insides, and I was up sick all night. Needless to say, I flushed the rest of the brandy, and I kept the small putty container as a souvenir of my rule-breaking Dad.

As for the rest of the decorations, I still have some of them as they remain some of my favorite holiday decorations, filled with amazing memories and miracles. Mom sent me one of those silly singing Christmas trees and this amazing Christmas tree advent calendar that sat on a pedestal of twenty-four little drawers, each filled with one ornament. When I plugged in the tree, it rotated, played music, and changed colors. I had never seen anything like it before, and it was perfect as it focused my attention.

As I was opening both boxes, I felt angry and disappointed. The more I opened, the more upset I felt. Then, as I unwrapped the box with the Advent tree—that had a sign to open before December 1—I felt and heard in my head that nothing was going to change the fact that I was going to be in Kuwait for Christmas.

As I set up that Advent tree, I realized I had a choice. I could continue to feel upset and angry, or I could choose to make the very best of the situation.

I was reminded of a Byron Katie quote:

When I argue with reality, I lose, but only 100 percent of the time.

From that point on, I did everything I could to make the most of my reality. Mom sent everything to make a beautiful wreath along with several other decorations for my office space. I told another co-worker, MaryBeth, about the care packages, so after Thanksgiving dinner, she and I took all the decorations to the office. We created a wreath using the ornaments and festive ribbon Mom included. We set up the singing Christmas tree, strung lights and tinsel, and made the office jolly and cheerful.

When everyone returned to work the next day, they all commented on how joyful and merry the space felt. I discovered the decorations lifted everyone's spirits, and together, we embraced the reality that we were stuck in Kuwait for the holidays. Together, we committed to making it the best we could.

As I progressed more and more into the season, I thought of other ways to increase my enjoyment. It occurred to me that I could find a way to keep some of our family traditions while being apart. One of our traditions is to go to midnight mass on Christmas Eve. It turned out MaryBeth also sang in the church choir, and she invited me to attend midnight mass.

Her invitation gave me the idea to figure out a way to have our traditional breakfast on Christmas. In our house, we enjoy fried dough for breakfast every Christmas morning. It is called *pizza fritta*, and it is the only day of the year we have this special treat. All I needed was some fresh dough. I devised a plan to go to the pizza place in our food court and ask for a ball of fresh pizza dough before they baked it into a pizza.

Acquiring dough proved to be quite an adventure due to the language barrier. The employees at the pizza restaurant could not understand why I wanted the raw dough and eventually acquiesced, but they would only give me the dough already stretched into the pizza pan, not a ball of dough. They handed me the entire pizza pan, and through broken English and hand and arm signals, made me promise to bring the pan back. I brought the pan and dough to my trailer, took the dough out of the pan, placed it into a plastic bag, and put it in the refrigerator. I immediately washed the pan and returned it to the pizza workers who were still looking at me with complete confusion and wonder. Mission accomplished.

The real miracle began to take shape within a day or two of my choice to do my best to enjoy the holidays. I received a cryptic message from my mentor's wife Willie, asking me to keep my ears to the ground because Bruce, her husband and my first mentor in the Army, might be passing though Kuwait for the holidays. At that time, my mentor was serving as a senior military aide in the Pentagon to an Under Secretary. I supposed the Under Secretary was going to travel to the area to support troops during the holidays. I wrote back that I understood the message and would keep my ear to the ground.

I then walked to another office that would know if there were any senior leaders planning to visit Kuwait for the holidays. They were surprised I knew about it and told me that they did expect to receive a senior leader on Christmas night. Eventually, as the time drew closer, I was in direct contact with Bruce, who was able to tell me when and where they would be spending Christmas night.

He then asked if I could come to the hotel for Christmas dinner. I was ecstatic. I then asked Bob if he would be willing to drive to the hotel with me on

Christmas. Due to security protocols, we had to travel in pairs, have a weapon with us in the vehicle, and have a letter signed by a colonel allowing the trip into the city. He said yes, it would be his pleasure. I then had to muster up the courage to ask our boss, the colonel who had to sign the memo, if he would authorize an evening trip into Kuwait City.

I waited until we were all together having a little office celebration. I had learned early it is best to ask tough questions when folks are in a good mood. I explained the entire situation to my boss, and he said yes. He asked to speak to Bob to make sure he was really okay with giving up his Christmas night to help me. Bob said it would be his honor with sincere sentiment.

I was so excited my entire body tingled, and I sent an email to Bruce's wife to let her know that I had permission to meet Bruce for Christmas dinner. Willie wrote back and said that while she was sad to spend Christmas without him, she was grateful he would have an opportunity to break bread with me on Christmas.

When Christmas Eve came, I did attend a special midnight service and enjoyed the beautiful music of the choir. Before going to sleep that night, I took out the pizza dough to let it rise as my mother always did when we got home from midnight mass. On Christmas morning, I woke up, excited to make pizza fritta for the first time in my life. It was delicious and helped me appreciate all our holiday traditions.

It may seem silly, but that food brought me closer to my family in spite of the physical distance and time difference. I enjoyed a leisurely morning and early afternoon eating pizza fritta and opening my stocking that Mom sent completely packed full of goodies all the way to Kuwait.

Christmas afternoon came and, after enjoying an early dinner with our entire office at the dining facility, my boss wished me a safe trip to Kuwait City. I was so excited and in complete awe that all of this unfolded in such an incredible and unexpected way.

Bob and I arrived at the hotel about twenty minutes before Bruce, so I was in the lobby when he arrived. There was a strict security protocol at the entrance of the hotel, so once Bruce came through security, we walked towards each other. It was such a special moment in time that neither of us ever imagined would happen when we first met ten years before. He was my second battalion commander when I was a new second lieutenant, and he and his wife played a significant role in my development as an officer and as a lady.

Bruce went upstairs to put his bags away, and when he returned, he asked about the eating options at the hotel. Ironically, their signature steak house restaurant was closed for renovations, and the only restaurant available in the hotel was their Japanese restaurant. Bruce invited Bob to join us for dinner, and Bob refused saying he was prepared to use the time to study for his professional engineer license. We both insisted that Bob join us, but he would not. I could tell Bob didn't want to intrude and was genuinely looking forward to the opportunity to study.

I had never had sushi for Christmas dinner before, and I didn't care. I was breaking bread with my mentor. It was a lovely evening filled with catching up, mentoring, and laughter. At the time, I was spending many nights questioning if I would stay in the Army. I was in love at that time and didn't want to be away from my loved one.

I remember Bruce saying that he didn't always love being in the military, and there were times when he loved it one year at a time. That approach moved him closer to his next assignment or next promotion. I never forgot that conversation, especially any time I found myself not loving the job or location. It was not lost on me that all of this had unfolded after I made the decision to change my attitude about spending my first Christmas away from home.

Is it possible all those miracles would have happened if I remained angry and sad? I guess, but I have come to understand that when I shut down parts of myself, it becomes difficult for the universe to provide support. It can only give me what I focus my attention on. By shifting all of my attention on making the very best of a not-so-great situation, the universe responded in kind and went beyond what I could ever imagine.

If anyone told me when I deployed to Kuwait that I would enjoy Christmas dinner with Bruce in downtown Kuwait City, I would have said, "That's ridiculous. That's impossible."

When you change your attitude and make a different choice, the universe shifts with you. Choose wisely and remain in awe and curiosity as paths you never imagined open with complete ease and grace.

Journal Exercise

1. Is there a time in your life when you chose a different attitude or perspective? If so, what was the outcome?

CHAPTER 19

ASK FOR WHAT YOU WANT

In the military, when it was time for me to complete one assignment and begin another, my assignment officer asked me to submit my top choices. The assignment officer was responsible for handing out the new assignments and sent out a list of all the open positions across the globe. Over the years, several assignment officers asked me that same question using many different methods. One asked for my top three choices; another asked for my top five choices and bottom two choices. One assignment officer created an excel spreadsheet that required me to select my top twenty choices from a drop-down menu. That one made me giggle because of its complexity.

Because it was my best opportunity to get a location and a job that I really desired, I filled it out exactly as instructed. At the end of the day, it is important to note that the needs of the Army will always come first. Yet, I was always hopeful each time I sent in my top choices.

For me, I felt empowered and listened to when asked as someone cared about what was most important to me. Still, there was one request I never made until my guide on this earth, my sister, spoke one simple statement to me: *Ask for what you want.*

Before I share the rest of the story, I will share that prior to my sister's advice on this subject and even after, I heard the same thing said many ways. For example, my spiritual mentor Debra Poneman talked about asking for what you want in terms of ordering from a catalog. In her example, she used a department store catalog. (Or a more updated example: How does Amazon know what to deliver until you go into the app and order what you want?) Debra went on to explain that it is the same with the universe. Until you ask for what you want, the universe or the God of your understanding cannot deliver anything.

Even with that knowledge—what request had I never made? I never asked, not once in nineteen years of service, for an assignment to my birthplace—Hawaii. Besides being my birthplace, my parents bought their first home there and never sold it. They moved back to it after renting it out for thirty years, and I wanted to be close to them. As you might imagine, Hawaii was a popular assignment: an opportunity to live on a tropical island for three years while someone else pays for the plane ticket.

In 2010, I was sent to Afghanistan for a year-long deployment and was talking to my sister about my options for my assignment after Afghanistan. I told her I really wanted to go to Hawaii, but the chances of me landing that assignment were slim because everyone wanted Hawaii.

She said to me, "Anela, they can't say yes *or* no if you don't ask them."

Such a simple yet profound statement. For all those years of my career, I had told myself the same thing repeatedly: *I can't ask for what I really want because everyone is asking for the same thing.* If that were true, then wouldn't we all drive the exact same car and buy the exact same style house in the same location? We all have our own likes and dislikes, yet I had convinced myself that everyone must be asking to move to Hawaii, so I didn't bother to ask because I wouldn't get it anyway. I had never given the military the chance to say yes or no. Worse yet, I had already done their thinking and made the decision for them.

Then in December 2010, my assignment officer told us there were seventy of us needing to move in the summer of 2011, and he provided us with the list of all the available assignments and their locations. I was ecstatic to discover there were a total of five open positions in Hawaii. My assignment officer asked us to list our top five choices and our bottom two choices. I looked at all the jobs in Hawaii and listed: #1 Hawaii, #2 Hawaii, #3 Hawaii, #4 Korea, and #5? You guessed it. Hawaii! I was fairly certain they wouldn't send me to another one-year assignment coming out of Afghanistan, so my #4 was really a throw away choice and my way of showing I was a team player. I researched all the job titles in Hawaii and decided my #3 choice would have the highest learning curve, and given my background, I was among a small group of qualified officers for that job.

That's right! The very first time I asked for Hawaii (after nineteen years of service), I got my first choice for location and my third choice of job assignments. I thought: *Really? The first time I ask, the Army says yes? Heck! Why didn't I ask nineteen years ago, ten years ago, five years ago?*

When I arrived in Hawaii in 2011, I met soldiers who received assignments to Hawaii two and three times during their career because they did ask, and not everyone wants to live in Hawaii. It was such an invaluable life lesson, and I have since mentored many other people using the same wise advice when wondering if they should or shouldn't ask for what they want.

Remember—the person you are asking can't say yes or no if you don't ask. In fact, by default, the answer is no when you don't bother to ask.

So do not ever be afraid to ask for what you want. You might just be surprised and get it.

Journal Exercise

1. What do you want?
2. Have you asked for it? If not, what's stopping you?

CHAPTER 20

THE END

There really is no end, just the continuation of this journey called life. Why all of these stories? For me, each lesson I learned shaped me into the person I am today. The more I put these lessons into consistent daily practice, the more becoming all I can be emerges.

No matter the traumas you have experienced, no matter when you start (it is never too late), you have the power to choose your next step.

I believe we are here to live our lives from a place of love, from a place of the very best version of ourselves. What I have come to discover is it takes consistent awareness, constant vigilance, and continual growth to become the best version of myself. While I have taken many great courses and read even more great personal growth books, it wasn't until I committed to a year-long program, hired two coaches and an energy practitioner, and met bi-weekly with a group of like-minded women to hold intentions for each other that I began to see tangible shifts in my life.

I also took up meditation and found peace in the fact that life is a journey, not a destination. The more I discover, the more I expand, the more there is to discover—and the more expanding there is to do. While many of the steps and techniques I followed might be simple, doing them consistently was hard for me until I created a strong support team around myself.

I continue to be a work in progress, and I am no longer striving to find *the* destination. For years, I expected that if I did all this inner work, I would one day *arrive*. I would *make it*. In my experience, there is no *getting* there. It is one big, wonderous unfolding adventure.

We are meant to go with the flow. After incorporating each of the lessons in this book into my daily life, I am now much quicker to see and feel when I am not in the flow of life. This awareness is yet another gift for becoming all I can be because now I stop trying to force things. Instead, I release my hold on whatever it is I am pursuing and return to floating with the river instead of constantly fighting to swim upstream.

One of my greatest joys is witnessing others when the proverbial light bulb comes on. I learned a long time ago that I love a story, and long after an event or book might end, it is the story and the lesson in that story that sticks with me.

This is my hope in writing this book. If just one story I shared gives you a new perspective, a new way to look at something, and that new way brings you more joy or peace—then sharing my story is worth it. By sharing some of my trials and tribulations in becoming all I can be, I hope you are inspired to continue on your path of becoming all you can be. By shining my light, I want you to feel empowered to shine your light as well.

Together, we will add to the overall light in the world.

If so called, I would be honored to be a part of your support team on your path to becoming all you can be. Stay tuned for the next book, where I share the journey of transitioning from becoming all you can be to being all you can be. There is no end; there are only new beginnings.

CONTACT THE AUTHOR

Download a copy of your *Becoming All You Can Be:*
A Companion Journal at:
www.AnelaArcari.com

Connect with Anela Arcari:
LinkedIn: @AnelaArcari
Website: www.anelaarcari.com

Please Post a Review

If you like what you read in *Becoming All You Can Be,* please post a review at your favorite online retailer. This will help me reach more people and share this message.

Thank you.

Acknowledgments

What an incredible journey! Writing a chapter in *Turning Point Moments* was fairly easy when compared to writing a whole book. When I decided to go with Christine Kloser and her *Get Your Book Done Accelerator* program, I believed her when she said the process of writing the book would transform me. And it has!

I wish to thank my parents who love and stand by me no matter what ideas I come up with. I am especially grateful for my dad's service in the Army and my mother's service as a proud Army spouse and proud Army mom. Their love of travel and enthusiasm for every adventure gave me my wanderlust. I love you, and no number of words can adequately express my gratitude for everything you sacrificed for and provided to me.

There is no doubt in my mind that my sister and I picked each other long before we came into this current form. I have often referred to her as my biggest fan, cheerleader, and guide on this earth. She opened my eyes to so many wonderful concepts growing up, and I am eternally grateful. Thank you for all your love and support. I can't wait to see where our paths take us next.

To everyone I mention in this book: I know some of your names, others I do not, but each of you and many more played a key role in my life. These stories are just the tip of the iceberg of tales I can tell about my life growing up and serving in the military. Thank you for allowing me to include you in this first book.

There are coaches and energy practitioners who help me on a weekly basis to stay focused, centered, and present. Leila Reyes, Gerise Pappas, Colleen Campbell, and Joy Taylor hold space for me and play vital roles in my becoming all I can be. Thank you for your love, consistent insights, sage advice, and unwavering dedication to helping others become all they can be.

To the many Army brats I grew up with and met during my father's career and to all the soldiers and friends I served with during my career—*Thank You!* Each of you is a string in the fabric of the story of my life, and I am forever grateful for your sacrifice and service. It was an honor to serve alongside you and to serve our nation especially: Chris, CaS, Estee, Joan, and Dawn. A special thank you to Jim who first saw this book in 2000: Thank you for sharing that vision and holding space for this version to be born.

To my first tribes that formed at Mercy High School and Norwich University. The women of the Class of 1987 from Mercy High School whom I call the *Mercy Girls* were my first tribe, and I am grateful that we are connecting on a regular basis, thanks to COVID. The men of the Class of 1991 from Norwich University that

I call my *Big Brothers*: Thank you for your friendship and love, and for protecting me then and now.

I wrote about the start of my own consistent spiritual journey that began in 2018 in my chapter in *Turning Point Moments*. It began with *Your Year of Miracles*, and I still participate in it today. I am grateful to Marci Shimoff, Debra Poneman, Dr. Sue Morter, and Lisa Garr as well as the many amazing leaders in the world of personal transformation they have as guests in the program. A special thank you to my *Yes to Success* roommate, Andrea, and all my Miracle Sisters who walk by my side on this journey of becoming all we can be.

A special shout out to the incredible writers, Nancy, Mary, Val, and Elizabeth I met and shared some of these stories with in my first writing group during COVID. Thank you for your honest feedback and, more importantly, for your encouragement to get these stories out into the world. I am grateful to each of you and look forward to reading your stories.

I wish to thank Christine Kloser and her entire team at *Get Your Book Done Accelerator* and Capucia Publishing, LLC. In particular Christine, David, Jean, Carrie, Karen, Harriet, and Penny for all their patience with me as I started a new job, moved across the country, and then left the job in the middle of writing this book. I also send light and love to all the amazing women who participated in the June 2022–May 2023 cohort—a powerful circle of women I call soulmates. I am honored to be publishing alongside you.

To the most amazing and talented photographer, Lauren Mudrock, who took the incredible photos for this book, my website, and social media. I never knew a photo shoot could be so much fun. Thanks to Christine's team for sharing her information!

A big thank you to you, the reader of this book. I pray you have found it helpful and enjoyable, and that you are inspired to shine your light while becoming all you can be.

References

Better Homes and Gardens. 1963. *Meals with a Foreign Flair.* New York: Meredith Press.

Freedom Writers Foundation. "Our Story." *Freedom Writers Foundation.* www.Freedomwritersfoundation.org/about

About the Author

Anela Arcari is a combat engineer veteran with twenty-eight years of service turned intuitive, mystical coach and mentor. A two-time Amazon best-selling contributing author and executive producer of a transformational documentary,  Anela's innate gifts elicit the best transformation for her clients. She is a highly recommended and sought-after leadership and personal growth coach, speaker, and mentor.

Her experiences growing up in a military family and serving in the military inform her unique experiences and perspectives that fuel her drive in becoming all she can be and helping others in becoming all they can be.

Anela lives in Brooklyn, New York, and holds a MS in Education (Leadership Development and Counseling) and is a National Certified Counselor (NCC).

ALSO BY ANELA ARCARI

"Say Yes to You" (chapter) in *Turning Point Moments: True Inspirational Stories About Creating a Life that Works for You* Capucia Publishing, 2022

"Take the First Step" (chapter) in *The Power and Impact of Courageous Changemakers Stories of Life, Love, and Business* Hybrid Global Publishing, 2024